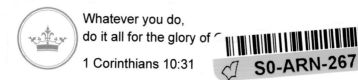
Debra,

You are a light and a joy
to so many. Thank you for
serving the Lord with joy.

Nancy Greener
8/2014

Eyewitness to a Savior

Experience the Life of Jesus Christ

Nancy Elizabeth Gainor

CROSSBOOKS
PUBLISHING

CrossBooks™
A Division of LifeWay
1663 Liberty Drive
Bloomington, IN 47403
www.crossbooks.com
Phone: 1-866-879-0502

Images captured and created by Haley Thaxton Gainor, Laura Michelle Gainor, and Mary Frances Gainor

Scripture taken from the HOLY BIBLE, NEW INTERNATIONAL VERSION® Copyright © 1973, 1978, 1984 Biblica. Used by permission of Zondervan. All rights reserved.

First published by CrossBooks   05/29/2014

ISBN: 978-1-4627-3746-8 (sc)
ISBN: 978-1-4627-3747-5 (hc)
ISBN: 978-1-4627-3745-1 (e)

Library of Congress Control Number: 2014908974

Printed in the United States of America.

This book is printed on acid-free paper.

Dedicated to Jesus Christ,
who whispered these
words of inspiration into my heart.

Preface

The poems in this book are based on the Scriptures. Verbiage and imagery are purely the imagination of the author. This manuscript was written for two purposes. The first and foremost is to honor God. As my fingers race across the keyboard and the words flow effortlessly on the page, I believe I serve as a conduit in delivering God's message to touch lives and turn hearts toward Him. Secondly, the composition reflects the dedication of my time and talents to serve a merciful Lord in a ministry that I pray is widespread. I hope this book prompts the reader to pursue a personal relationship with a loving God who is alive and active today.

Acknowledgments

I am very grateful to my loving husband, John Gainor, who encourages me and is so supportive of this ministry. What a blessing to walk this life journey with my best friend!

I am thankful to my sons, Michael, Brian, and Daniel Gainor, who promote confidence and enthusiasm.

This book is greatly enhanced by the creative photographs provided by my talented and lovely "daughters," Haley, Laura, and Mary Gainor.

I appreciate the boundless love and joy instilled by my adorable grandchildren, Kendall, Clara, Grayson, and Garrett.

I am indebted to the passionate endorsement of family and friends who have been my loyal supporters.

My greatest tribute is to my Savior, for He alone provides the inspiration and the means to get the job done. Praise and honor to God!

Arrival

The Chosen One

Gripping the coarse
edge of the basin,
Mary gingerly lifts
the swirling water
from the abundant well.
Turning to leave, an
extraordinary vision
awaits, causing the
precious cargo to slip
from her trembling hands.
Etched in light, the angel's
lucid eyes, wisp of
golden hair, and flowing
opal robe transcend
an air of purity, holiness,
kindness, and peace.
Gabriel, the messenger,
has arrived to address
Mary, the chosen one.
This modest girl, surging
with humility, goodness,
love, and abundant faith,
has been selected to be
the mother of Jesus Christ.

Lacking a formative education,
royal lineage, or even a
husband, the virgin seems
an unlikely candidate for
this daunting position.
Yet, God appreciates her
righteous qualifications.
The miraculous conception will
alter the life of this young girl.
At this significant moment,
Mary does not concentrate
on the fear of rejection or
condemnation; instead
she voices praiseworthy
songs that reflect her
respectful stance for
this esteemed position.
Mary's courage and
praise in the face of
adversity illustrate how
we should approach the
challenges God plants
within our faith garden.

But the angel said to her, "Do not be afraid, Mary; you have found favor with God. You will conceive and give birth to a son, and you are to call him Jesus." (Luke 1:30–31 New International Version)

Kindred Spirits

Two cousins embrace
within an arched doorway,
reunited after years
of separation, and blissful
to see one another.
The cords that bind
these women together
are not just genealogically
fastened, for they share an
incredible connection:
Both are with child. Moreover,
there is nothing ordinary about
their circumstances, for God's
masterful plan has woven
these miracle births together.
Mary, young and virginal,
has conceived a child through
the Holy Spirit, and Elizabeth,
aged and barren, is expecting
a child as well. Additionally,
both birth announcements
were angelically foretold.
As they clutch one another,
Elizabeth's baby stirs in her
    womb.
Instantly, it is revealed to her
that Mary is carrying the
    Messiah.
With tear-filled eyes, she
    celebrates
the ecstatic revelation with the
one she loves. Thus, the burden
of secrecy Mary bears is lifted
as God provides friendship and
support for the ostracized
heroines who desperately
need one another. Mary
and Elizabeth, kindred
spirits who are forever
bound by the love of God.

In a loud voice she exclaimed: "Blessed are you among women, and blessed is the child you will bear!" (Luke 1:42NIV)

The Taxing Journey

Joseph's eyes fixate
on his expectant fiancée.
Approvingly, he beholds
his radiant love whose
sun-kissed cheeks,
sparking brown eyes,
and soft smile reveal
her inner bliss as the
mother of God's Son.
Basking in contentment,
Joseph's mind momentarily
escapes the disdain and
criticism of his peers due
to their perceived "immoral
behavior." His focus now
is on the welfare of his
future wife and baby.
The impending trip to
Bethlehem to register
for the Roman census and the
subsequent taxes haunts him.
Mary's delicate condition
is threatened by this
dangerous expedition.
Prayerfully, Joseph entrusts
his family's fate to his
protective heavenly Father.
Stoically, he leads a donkey,
with Mary astride, as they
embark upon a journey of faith.
Fulfilling God's purpose for
our lives is not always easy;
however, we can always trust
His sovereign presence
and abiding love.

So Joseph also went up from the town of Nazareth in Galilee to Judea, to Bethlehem the town of David, because he belonged to the house and line of David. He went there to register with Mary, who was pledged to be married to him and was expecting a child. (Luke 2:4–5 NIV)

Proclamation

Dusk is approaching, and a
chill filters through
the worn, linen wrap
of a lonely shepherd who
is guiding his flock along
the ridge of a ragged hill.
Tufts of grass amidst the
parched, pressed dirt
regale the brigade and
allow a moment of rest
for its weary inhabitants.
As the shepherd surveys the
horizon, he is struck by the
seemingly endless hills that
appear to unravel into the
distance as far as he can see.
This is the only life He has
ever known, for this skill
was passed down from
generation to generation.
Uneducated but highly skilled,
he vows to protect his sheep
and tends to their needs.
Haggard and aged, the lonely
shepherd has endured years of
monotony, fluctuating weather,

the danger of animal attacks,
as well as exhaustion from
trekking boundless trails.
Nothing extraordinary has
ever occurred during the
countless years on his watch.
As the sun descends and
the moon rises, it looks as if
the countless stars will
once again offer him
companionship throughout
the dark hours of the night.
This evening, one star
in particular illuminates
the sky in a brilliant blaze
and appears to target
its radiance to a specific
location nearby.
Suddenly, in the stillness,
thousands of figures
appear, silhouetted by
the moonlight and
translucent in nature.
The songs descending
from the heavens compel
the astonished witness to

his knees in reverent prayer for this remarkable display of God's great and powerful glory. As he does so, one of the angels addresses him and says, "Do not be afraid, I bring you good news of great joy, for today in the town of David, a Savior has been born to you; He is Christ the Lord." God's message declaring the birth of Jesus did not extend to royalty or political figureheads; instead, it was designed specifically to be received by an ordinary shepherd on a hillside. How amazing!

And there were shepherds living out in the fields nearby, keeping watch over their flocks at night. An angel of the Lord appeared to them, and the glory of the Lord shone around them, and they were terrified. But the angel said to them, "Do not be afraid. I bring you good news that will cause great joy for all the people. Today in the town of David a Savior has been born to you; he is the Messiah, the Lord. This will be a sign to you: You will find a baby wrapped in cloths and lying in a manger." (Luke 2:8–12 NIV)

Encapsulated Moment

Huddled together for warmth, Mary and Joseph delight in the moonlit glow. The sheltered stable's inky darkness is pierced by a sterling star's radiant beam that caresses the sleeping newborn, Jesus. The crunch of frayed straw settles beneath the parents' feet, and the lulling murmur of animals resonates in this unlikely delivery room. Exhausted and exhilarated, Mary's wet locks trickle droplets down her flushed cheeks. The intense pain that seared her body is now a distant memory, lost in the vision of her beautiful baby grasping her finger with His minuscule hand. Diverting her gaze to Joseph, she lovingly recalls his reaction to the birth process. Throughout the ordeal, Joseph's tender concern was endearing. Smiling, Mary remembers his frantic albeit quick-witted negotiations with the begrudging innkeeper. During these moments of uncertainty, God's provision and promise offered Mary serenity. Crouched by her side, for her sake Joseph had masked his fear and uttered words of reassurance as well as prayer. God provided a devout husband committed to protect and support Mary in her time of need. As her lips brush the silky hair of her precious babe, Mary marvels at the privilege of being the mother of God's holy Son. Although an uncertain future beckons, time stands still during this encapsulated moment. This enthralling glimpse showcases a family entwined in love and faith, captivated by each other and blessed by their heavenly Father.

While they were there, the time came for the baby to be born, and she gave birth to her firstborn, a son. She wrapped him in cloths and placed him in a manger, because there was no guest room available for them. (Luke 2:6, 7 NIV)

$\mathcal{R}$everence

Eyes directed to the heavenly stars
with hearts drawn to the Almighty,
the three astronomers sense a calling.
Having read the biblical prophecies,
studied celestial patterns, and engaged
in fervent prayer, a decision transpires.
Preparations are made to begin a
quest to locate the Messiah, sent by God,
who will save His people. Provisions are
packed and placed upon the strong
backs of dromedaries that will
transport these travelers to their
destination. Their compass? A star rising
up from the east determining the way.
Thus they proceed into the unknown,
trusting a light sent by the great I AM.
Heads hung low, clutching the coarse hair
of the bellowing camels, they venture
across a rough coastline, dipping into
marshy valleys, climbing rugged ridges,
and zigzagging across arid deserts.
They navigate for months until an encounter
with King Herod exposes their mission.
Alas, the shifting luminosity rests upon
a tiny babe and His parents. Offering gifts
of gold (kingship), frankincense (deity),

and myrrh (suffering), the three wise men drop
to their knees in reverence to their Savior,
God's precious Son, Jesus. Come, let us too
worship our redeemer, priest, and king, our
very own Messiah in all His glory. Alleluia!

When they saw the star, they were overjoyed. On coming to the house,
they saw the child with his mother Mary, and they bowed down and
worshiped him. Then they opened their treasures and presented him
with gifts of gold, frankincense and myrrh. (Matthew 2: 10–11 NIV)

Dreaming

Lost in a state
of unconsciousness,
Joseph has finally
succumbed to a
profoundly deep sleep.
Family obligations,
emotional stress, and
painful toil have
produced a state
of near-exhaustion.
Abruptly interrupting
his vacant thoughts, a
blurry image of an
angel materializes,
invoking a clear
message: "Get up and
take the child and his
mother to Egypt, for
Herod is searching for
the child to kill him."
Without hesitation,
Joseph gathers his
family and vanishes
into a veil of darkness.
Subsequent dreams
would dictate similar
instructions regarding
noteworthy destinations.
Obediently, Joseph
submits to God's will,
and the prophecies
regarding the Messiah's
origin and ethnicity
are ultimately fulfilled.
God's reasoning is never
questioned by Joseph,
and his complaints
are nonexistent as he
abides the directives
specified within three
distinctive dreams.
Just as a blind man is
led by one who has
sight, so we too can
trust our protective
guide, Jesus Christ.

When they had gone, an angel of the Lord appeared to Joseph in a dream. "Get up." he said, "Take the child and his mother and escape to Egypt. Stay there until I tell you, for Herod is going to search for the child and kill him." (Matthew 2:13 NIV)

Dedication

As Mary and Joseph carefully
tread up the worn stone steps
of the temple, the child Jesus
marvels at the beauty of the
massive structure. Even at
a tender age, He understands
the importance of this
holy place of worship, and
He knows this will be a
significant day in His life.
The ritualistic ceremony
of presenting their child
to the Lord demonstrates
the obedient nature of
Mary and Joseph. Passing
through the Huldah Gates
that lead to the sanctuary,
they enter a silent room.
Only their footsteps are
heard as they proceed
to the impressive altar.
Clothed in a charcoal robe
with a draped, pallid shawl,
the rabbi begins the litany
concerning commitment,
obligation, trust, and service.
As the words resonate in
her heart, Mary reflects
on her responsibility
parenting the Son of God.
Vowing to devote herself
daily to God's desire, she
pledges to support Jesus as He
follows the will of His Father.
God's divine plan surpasses
anything she can ever
imagine, but Mary surrenders
the destiny of her child
to His almighty Creator.

When the time came for the purification rites required by the Law of Moses, Joseph and Mary took him to Jerusalem to present him to the Lord. (Luke 2:22 NIV)

Childhood

A Lost Son

The weary parents are
anticipating their return
to the comfortable and serene
surroundings they call home.
The Feast of the Passover
in Jerusalem has been
exhilarating, for it was a
time to renew their
commitment to God,
offer worshipful praise,
and reunite with family and
friends. They were excited
to introduce Jesus, now a
budding youth of twelve, to
the ceremonious customs
of the temple and allow Him
to observe doctrinal
discussions.
It had been a day into the
lengthy trip and Mary assumed
Jesus was trailing with His
cousins,
caught up in the merriment of
youthful compatibility.
In a panic, she discovers the
devastating news that He is
nowhere to be found! Tears begin
to gush as she anguishes over
the many scenarios she
envisions happening to her
cherished son. Joseph holds her
close, devastated to hear her
muffled cries, and vows to
retrieve their one and only child.
Scrambling to gather their
    provisions,
they return to Jerusalem with lips
quivering and prayers uttered
along the way. Fear grips their
hearts, for this city poses potential
harm to their beloved. Guilt
saturates their thoughts as the
parents analyze their actions
and question their ability to
be adequate custodians to
this exceptional child. Queries
flow incessantly.
Where could He be? Why didn't
we watch Him more closely?
Where do we begin to look
    for Him?
Drawn to the temple courts, their

apprehension fades as Jesus' voice gravitates toward them. Here is the boy, pivotally placed within a nucleus of distinguished observers. The teachers are
actually
posing questions and receiving responses laden with profound intellect beyond their
comprehension.
As the harrowing tale is divulged, Jesus simply asks why had they not known that He would be in His father's house? Mary collects all these things in her heart.
United
in a blend of deity and
humanity, Christ
empathizes with us, and
furthermore
He offers us salvation—for He is not the lost one; we are.

After three days they found him in the temple courts, sitting among the teachers, listening to them and asking them questions. Everyone who heard him was amazed at his understanding and his answers. (Luke 2:46–47 NIV)

Home

Nazareth is the town
Jesus calls His home.
It is here where He dwells
in a house embedded in laughter.
Here multiple siblings interact
amidst a flurry of household tasks
as well as jubilant play in the street.
Habitual trips are made to the
synagogue where neighborhood
rabbis offer wisdom and guidance.
The clamor of the marketplace is
clothed in a sachet of ripened
fruit and herbs dangling in the breeze.
Multigenerational relatives convene
in prayer over a table covered with
a meal painstakingly prepared with love.
Families occupy a sparse residence
where the basic provisions are sufficient.
The thriving venue of Nazareth is the
backdrop for Jesus' formative years.
Intermingled in the community,
He appears to be just a boy and
then a young man learning a trade.
Oblivious to His true identity, the
citizens of this municipality
actually interact regularly

with the Son of God.
Predictions allege that the
Messiah will emerge from
this seemingly insignificant city.
Jesus, our Messiah, transforms
the lives of those who seek His
presence. Let Him create a home
in your heart forever.

When Joseph and Mary had done everything required by the Law of
the Lord, they returned to Galilee to their own town of Nazareth.
And the child grew and became strong; he was filled with wisdom,
and the grace of God was on him. (Luke 2:39–40 NIV)

'Nazareth! Can anything good come from there?" Nathanael asked.
"Come and see," said Philip, (John 1:46 NIV)

Labor of Love

His hands glide
across the smooth
surface of the sturdy
table He has masterfully
constructed. Blowing
lightly, the tiny fragments
of sawdust disperse,
revealing a glossy finish.
Swirling grains travel
through the plank
showcasing the timber's
natural beauty. As Jesus
scrutinizes the finished
project, He smiles,
recollecting His carpentry
apprenticeship. Joseph's
passion for the trade was
infectious. His father
delighted in creating an
intricate design as well as
executing the steps to
completion. Optimum
lumber was selected
as the colleagues
energetically perfected
their technique. Often
traveling for miles, they
enjoyed each other's
company as they walked
to neighboring cities to
rebuild damages inflicted
by the Romans. Later,
a home carpentry shop
would be fashioned.
Jesus surveys the
empty workshop,
void of His favorite
collaborator. For
several years now
He has worked alone.
Deriving gratification
from every endeavor, Jesus
persistently completes
each task knowing that the
fruit of His labor is pleasing
to God, His family, and
His community. Our
vocation may differ from
carpentry, but the lessons
Joseph taught Jesus
concerning tenacity, effort,
and attitude ring true today.

Isn't this the carpenter? Isn't this Mary's son and the brother of James, Joseph, Judas, and Simon? Aren't his sisters here with us?" And they took offense at him. (Mark 6:3 NIV)

Initiate

Launch

Rippling currents meander
 gently,
transporting the lucid Jordan
 River
to a destination unknown.
Lofty clouds partially conceal
the sun's diffused rays.
Along the bank, bursts of
yellow wildflowers interpose
the foliage's emerald carpet.
The silence is broken by
boisterous proclamations
hailing from John the Baptist.
Lengthy tangled hair and a
garb constructed of wild
animal pelts, he hardly
appears to be a spiritual
mentor, and yet he is chosen
by God to steer the Israelites
toward repentance, preparing
them for the coming Messiah.
John is overwhelmed when
he sees Jesus approach for

he recognizes Him to be
the prophesied Savior.
The commencement of
baptism for Jesus is not
meant for contrition; rather
it is a symbolic launch
into obedient servanthood.
As Jesus rises above
the swirling water, a
thunderous voice from
heaven prevails upon
the astonished spectators.
God's incredible approval
showers esteemed love
and delight upon His Son and
marks Jesus' divine identity.
We, too, can be launched
into obedient spiritual service.
Through repentance and
commitment we can begin
a marvelous journey with
our Messiah in control.

At that time Jesus came from Nazareth in Galilee and was baptized by John in the Jordan. (Mark 1:9 NIV)

Parched

The desert, a vast wasteland of crumbled dirt,
is disintegrated by heat, drought, and insects.
A lifeless form that seems incessantly
hot, it has been devastated for years with
temperatures soaring by day as well as plunging
at night. Glimpses of life are rare in
this rugged terrain. Mirages have begun
appearing to the detached occupant who
imagines cooling streams of rushing
water as a respite from the oppressive
conditions. Jesus wanders through this
desert for forty horrendous days. His lack of
essential nourishment and hydration
have produced feebleness, a massive
headache, dripping brow, blurred vision,
and momentary blackouts. He longs
to rest His fatigued body, but the
extreme temperature fluctuation
prohibits this desire. As Satan converges
upon his prey, he confidently asserts the power
of temptation to sway our Lord during His weakest
moment. But Jesus understands His enemy, and
He comprehends what is needed to combat this
formidable rival. With God's strength, He will
be victorious. Our own battlefields are filled with
enticement, alluring lies, and empty promises.

However, we can prepare ourselves for these
confrontations by engaging in continuous
prayer, absorbing the Word, calling on
God for guidance, and always believing
His truth. When parched, we need only to seek
God's protection, and He will quench our spirit
and renew our strength to triumph over adversity.

At once the Spirit sent him out into the wilderness, and he was in the
wilderness forty days, being tempted by Satan. He was with the wild
animals, and angels attended him. (Mark 1:12–13 NIV)

King Jesus

The view from the temple is magnificent.
The utmost peak in the Holy City reveals
an expanse of structures nestled closely
together, separated by grimy thoroughfares
leading travelers in and out of its midst.
From this vantage point, Jesus can survey
the four corners of the metropolis
and observe the bustling activity
of its many occupants. This pinnacle
becomes the precipice from which Jesus
perches precariously, contemplating the
taunting of Satan, His adversary. "If you
are the Son of God throw yourself down,"
The prophesied Messiah is equated
with power and prestige. Feeding the
multitudes and performing miracles
are the characteristics expected from
this anticipated hero. Encouraging this
exploitation, Satan mocks Jesus and attempts to
entice Him to circumvent pain and suffering,
utilizing His clout to avoid the cross. In
contrast, our blessed Messiah comes to us
wrapped in love, obedience, humility,
selflessness, and compassion. The
authority manifested in our
Savior does not require advertisement,

violence, or exploitation. Our suffering servant sacrificed everything for us as He hung on the ordained cross for our sins. Our King Messiah reigns forever, triumphantly victorious, conquering His foe through the mighty power of love.

Then the devil took him to the holy city and had him stand on the highest point of the temple. 'If you are the Son of God," he said, "throw yourself down. For it is written: "'He will command his angels concerning you, and they will lift you up in their hands, so that you will not strike your foot against a stone.'"(Matthew 4:5–6 NIV)

Casting the Net

A burly and bronzed fisherman
releases his tightly clenched fist,
and the sturdy net is cast overboard.
Unsuspecting fish will soon swim
into its grasp, drawn from
familiar surroundings to the unknown.
Jesus perused the coastline, noting the
passion and exuberance of several
fisherman dutifully fulfilling their trade.
Conversing frequently with them concerning
matters of faith, Jesus knew that if He
would only ask, the anglers would follow him.
Abandoning everything, the fishermen will
depart from family, friends, job security, a
comfortable home, and journey into a
world that is unfamiliar, oppressive,
threatening, and arduous—all for the sake of a
stranger who seems to know them intimately.
There is something extraordinary about Jesus,
and His presence is intoxicating. The future
disciples marvel at the way this "outsider"
is able to seize their hearts, and they
easily became transfixed by His words
of wisdom, trusting Him with their lives.
"I will make you fishers of men," He claims.
Tossing out a net for fish is routine, but capturing

the hearts of men would certainly be a challenge.
By means of absolute trust they pursue and
obey the Son of God, impacting the lives of many.
The magnetism of Christ does not dim with time.
Today, we too can be hooked and released to
freedom because of the sacrificial love of Jesus Christ.

"Come, follow me," Jesus said, "and I will send you out to fish for people." At once they left their nets and followed him. (Matthew 4:19–20 NIV)

The First Miracle

Merry laughter, tapping feet,
harps and flutes sound the
splendor of celebratory music for
a young couple, so much in love,
hearts beating in unison.
Encircled by friends and family,
the gala of this wedding
has persisted for many days.
The finest wine that accompanies
succulent delicacies is quickly
dissipating, and the host is concerned.
Jesus arrives with His mother, Mary,
for this adored couple is family.
Immediately, He understands the alarm,
for without the wine, the embarrassment
of the bridegroom will ruin the affair.
Mary knows that Jesus' time of ministry
is at hand, and her encouragement
bolsters His waning confidence.
Per His instructions, heavy,
wide-brimmed stone vessels are
filled to capacity with well water.
Fixated on the fluid, the servants
are astonished to witness the clear
liquid transform into a burgundy hue.
The robust wine is lavished upon

unapprised wedding guests—and
thus the finest wine is served last.
Many did not witness this
incredible miracle. There was no
pomp and circumstance
or thunderous applause.
It was an intimate moment
capturing the adoration of
a father and His precious Son.
A manifestation of confidence
implanted to prepare Jesus
for future illustrations
of God's faithfulness.
In Cana, water became wine,
and Jesus became a masterful
example of the immense power
connected to obedient trust.

Jesus said to the servants, "Fill the jars with water"; so they filled them to the brim. (John 2:7 NIV)

What Jesus did here in Cana of Galilee was the first of the signs through which he revealed his glory; and his disciples believed in him. (John 2:11 NIV)

Bringing Down the House

The sounds are deafening.
Shouting, promoting, persuading,
arguing, screaming, and scolding
echo within the confines of the
Jerusalem temple courtyard.
The sanctuary that once embodied
a reverent silence now reverberates
with rowdiness, clamor, and
emotion. Each nook and cranny
is filled to capacity with money
changers, merchants, and nearly
three hundred thousand pilgrims
who have entered the holy site for
the celebration of Passover. Livestock
wander aimlessly without regard to
human obstacles. Cages containing doves
emit a putrid odor, and the combined bellows
of restrained cattle and sheep
add to the disarray. Aghast at the
site of this offensive use of his
Father's house, Jesus grabs some
cords, fabricating a whip. "He drove
all from the temple courts, both sheep
and cattle; He scattered the coins of
the money changers and overturned
their tables. To those who sold doves

He said, 'Get these out of here! Stop
turning my Father's house into a market!;
The Jews then responded to Him, 'What
sign can you show us to prove your
authority to do all this?' Jesus answered
them, 'Destroy this temple, and I will
raise it again in three days.' The
righteous anger of Christ prompts this
intense physical response. Foretelling
His death, Jesus equates His body with
the destroyed temple that will be
revived in three days. Christ lives
in you, and as a result your body is
His temple. How do you preserve the
holiness, credibility, love, and
forgiveness that is found within?
Scripture, prayer, and trust in God
will maintain this precious
edifice all your days, until it tumbles
and you ascend to heaven, God's
holy and perfect house of worship.

So he made a whip out of cords, and drove all from the temple courts, both sheep and cattle; he scattered the coins of the money changers and overturned their tables. To those who sold doves he said, "Get these out of here! Stop turning my Father's house into a market!" His disciples remembered that it is written: "Zeal for your house will consume me." The Jews then responded to him, "What sign can you show us to prove your authority to do all this?" Jesus answered them, "Destroy this temple, and I will raise it again in three days." They replied, "It has taken forty-six years to build this temple, and you are going to raise it in three days?" But the temple he had spoken of was his body. After he was raised from the dead, his disciples recalled what he had said. Then they believed the scripture and the words that Jesus had spoken. (John 2:15–22 NIV)

Ministry

Starting Over

Afraid and ashamed to be seen with Jesus, Nicodemus moves stealthily toward the dwelling where He resides, concealed by the thick layer of darkness deep into the night. Inside, an oil lamp shadows the wall, and Jesus eagerly welcomes the Pharisee ruler into the home. Christ understands that this visit is not vital to state affairs; rather, it is essential to matters of the heart. Nicodemus concedes that, based on observed miracles, Jesus' authority comes from God. Jesus replies, "'Very truly I
   tell you,
no one can see the kingdom of God unless they are born again.' 'How can someone be born when they are old?' Nicodemus asked." Our forgiving Lord is the source of the holiness that can spring eternal in you. Like the invisible wind, Christ's light exists and moves freely in those who believe. Upon receiving the Holy Spirit, your life is made new, and you are different than before, hence you are "born again." "For God so
   loved
the world that He gave His one
   and
only Son, that whoever believes
   in
Him shall not perish but have
   eternal
life. For God did not send His Son into the world to condemn the world, but to save the world
   through
Him." The starting line to
   salvation
originates with Christ. It is time to begin again: ready, set, go!

Jesus replied, "Very truly I tell you, no one can see the kingdom of God unless they are born again." "How can someone be born when they are old?" Nicodemus asked. "Surely they cannot enter a second time into their mother's womb to be born!" Jesus answered, "Very truly I tell you, no one can enter the kingdom of God unless they are born of water and the Spirit. Flesh gives birth to flesh, but the Spirit gives birth to spirit. You should not be surprised at my saying, 'You must be born again.'" (John 3:3–7 NIV)

For God so loved the world that he gave his one and only Son, that whoever believes in him shall not perish but have eternal life. For God did not send his Son into the world to condemn the world, but to save the world through him. Whoever believes in him is not condemned, but whoever does not believe stands condemned already because they have not believed in the name of God's one and only Son. (John 3:16–18 NIV)

Drink of the Living Water

This is not a chance meeting.
Perched atop a rocky hill,
a well lies in wait, providing
sustenance to a village below.
The Samaritan woman is at
the well drawing precious water,
an arduous chore she fulfills
    daily.
Suddenly, Jesus is at her side and,
astonishingly, He knows her by
    name.
In wonderment, she ponders the
the intimate details He knows
    concerning
her life, never truly understanding
that God is in her presence.
Furthermore, she observes that
although He is Jewish, He
    regards her
with kindness and familiarity.
She is mystified by this behavior,
because the relationship between
these two factions is often
adversarial and threatening.

The dialogue centers on the
crystal clear water dripping from
the urn used for transport.
Jesus clarifies that water
symbolizes the living spirit.
If she would ask for
a sip of this treasured
gift, God would inhabit her inner
being and alter her life forever.
Christ implores us to desire
a loving God who is sufficient for
all our needs, both physical and
    spiritual.
His Father adores those who
worship Him in spirit and truth.
Nothing is noteworthy except
the nourishment extracted
as we thirst for His Word and
a relationship dependent
    upon God.
The cool, refreshing liquid may
soothe our physical being,
but the heavenly living
water sustains our life.

Jesus answered her, "If you knew the gift of God and who it is that asks you for a drink, you would have asked him and he would have given you living water." (1 John 4:10NIV)

Believe

Is documented proof necessary for belief? Absolute faith drawn from the heart is our Lord's desire for us. Frustrated with the shallow faith of His fickle witnesses who demand validation of His deity, Jesus is tiring of their ultimatums. Yet, standing in His presence is an elected official of Herod once again asking for a miracle: to save the life of his terminal son.

Weary from travel, sunken eyes hinting at despair, hunched shoulders and a stooped head, he humbly falls at Christ's feet begging for mercy. Our compassionate healer responds, "Go home. Your son will live." Elated, the officer bounds to his horse, galloping twenty miles to Capernaum to embrace his son. Belief in this case did not materialize because of visionary proof, but evolved because a father's conviction stemmed from the trustworthy assurance of Christ.

The royal official said, "Sir, come down before my child dies." Go," Jesus replied, "your son will live." The man took Jesus at his word and departed. (John 4:49–50 NIV)

Interruption

It is the Sabbath, and the doors
of the temple in Capernaum close,
obstructing the echoes of an
active city and the distractions
that prevent focused worship.
Hushed voices soon subside as
all eyes converge upon the rabbi.
With authoritative intonation,
Jesus teaches God's truth to
a captive audience. Suddenly, in the
midst of the lesson, a possessed man
rises to his feet and interrupts
the orator by crying out, "What do
you want with us, Jesus of Nazareth?
Have you come to destroy us? I know
who you are—the Holy One of God!"
Satan has penetrated this quiet place of
devotion and has successfully distracted
the parishioners. The boisterous arrogance
of the trespasser creates fear and anxiety.
Satan loves to distort the truth to entice
the believer to have doubts, especially
concerning salvation. He acknowledges
that Jesus is the Holy One of God and
rightfully fears His presence. "Be quiet!'
said Jesus sternly. 'Come out of him!'

The impure spirit shook the man violently
and came out of him with a shriek."
Even the demons obey Christ, for He is
always victorious, and therefore we must place
our lives in His trustworthy hands. Hence,
the word quickly spread about Jesus' authority
as well as the marvels of His teaching. We,
however, do not need proof, signs, and wonders;
all we need to do is believe that He is Lord.

They went to Capernaum, and when the Sabbath came, Jesus went
into the synagogue and began to teach. The people were amazed at
his teaching, because he taught them as one who had authority, not
as the teachers of the law. Just then a man in their synagogue who
was possessed by an impure spirit cried out, "What do you want with
us, Jesus of Nazareth? Have you come to destroy us? I know who you
are—the Holy One of God!" "Be quiet!" said Jesus sternly. "Come
out of him!" The impure spirit shook the man violently and came
out of him with a shriek. (Mark 1:21–26 NIV)

Fever

Simon's mother-in-law anticipates
Jesus' visit with great delight. Her
daughter has shared stories of Simon's
adventures with the rabbi, and the
family enthusiastically welcomes
Him into their home. Abundant
preparations are instigated in
advance, including hours of preparing
succulent delicacies and cleaning
the home. In recent days, however,
a fever rages and renders her
weak and bedridden. News of her
illness spreads to Jesus. Lying helpless
in her bed, chills racing down her spine,
her head fuzzy and damp, she peeks
up at His compassionate face resting
above her own. Taking her hand, He
guides her to her feet. As she rises,
the fever vanishes and her health
is immediately restored. Energized,
she instantly is able to serve her
Lord and enjoy His company. Christ's
intervention is personal. A tender
touch suggests a closeness He desires
with those whom He sustains. The house
call symbolizes Jesus' availability within

the hearts and homes of those who trust
Him. The prayers issued within that home
make an impact. Andrew and Simon's
concern for their loved one brought
Jesus' attention to her bedside.
Be reassured that your prayers for
others also make a difference. Today,
let's praise our miraculous healer for
mending our mind, body, and soul!

As soon as they left the synagogue, they went with James and John to
the home of Simon and Andrew. Simon's mother-in-law was in bed
with a fever, and they immediately told Jesus about her. So he went
to her, took her hand and helped her up. The fever left her and she
began to wait on them. (Mark 1:29–31 NIV)

Rejected by His Own

Jammed into the synagogue,
family and friends of Jesus'
childhood pack the room.
The air is heavy with oppressive
heat and musty clothing.
Shoulder to shoulder they stand,
dusty sandals worn from travel,
minds wandering to chores curtailed;
abundant worries distract their attention.
Yet, in this moment, they want
to be obedient to God.
Standing for hours in His house,
they have come to worship their Creator
and reflect on His mighty Word.
Today is special because one of their
brothers, Jesus, is reading Isaiah.
Eyes fixed on the orator, all
are silent as Jesus' soothing voice
begins to reveal the truth.
"Today this scripture is
fulfilled in your hearing."
What would it be like
to have our Savior standing
in our presence reading God's truth?
Making Himself available for us?
Offering forgiveness and unconditional love?

Jesus knew their reaction would not
be favorable, appreciative, or accepting.
Angry voices, raised fists, and a
crescendo of threats shake
God's sacred abode as they
deny Christ as their Messiah.
He is rejected by his own.
Despite a history of miracles,
He is still considered just an
ordinary son of Mary and Joseph.
In fact, these neighbors want
to extinguish this light from heaven.
An opportunity is lost, forgiveness
and elevated joy is forsaken.
The rejection of loved ones
brings despair to one of their own.

Then he rolled up the scroll, gave it back to the attendant and sat down. The eyes of everyone in the synagogue were fastened on him. He began by saying to them, "Today this scripture is fulfilled in your hearing." (Luke 4:20–21 NIV)

The Catch

The gentle waters of the
Lake of Gennesaret splash
against the rugged and worn
planks of two vessels swaying
effortlessly with the prodding current.
Abandoned by fishermen rinsing their
nets, Jesus sees the boats as an
opportunity to teach a valuable lesson
to His disciples. Stepping over the stern
and onto the aged deck, He instructs
Simon to place the watercraft farther
from shore. Leaning against the
the heavy wooden oar, Jesus lowers
Himself upon a mound of bulky netting
and begins to teach. Afterward, Christ
instructs Simon to retreat to deeper
depths and let down his net. Complying,
Simon follows His directive somewhat
skeptically, as previous attempts to
catch fish have proven unsuccessful.
"Master, we've worked hard all night
and haven't caught anything. But
because you say so, I will let down
the nets." Released into the shoal

and stirred in circular motion, the
durable mesh becomes immediately
inundated with spiny, dorsal fin
musht. Abundant in number and
weighing up to two pounds each,
the substantial cargo causes
the net to stretch and tear.
A second boat follows suit,
and the captured treasure
triggers the mast to drift aft,
causing the craft to sink
from the weight of its bounty.
"When Simon Peter saw this,
he fell at Jesus' knees and said,
'Go away from me, Lord; I am a
sinful man!' Then Jesus said to Simon,
'Don't be afraid; from now on you
will fish for people.'" A lack of success
should not hinder our closeness with
God. Persevere and offer your petitions
to Jesus, knowing that He will provide
what is necessary to satisfy your heart,
soul, and mind and give you peace as
your destiny unravels in His hands.

When he had finished speaking, he said to Simon, "Put out into deep water, and let down the nets for a catch." Simon answered, "Master, we've worked hard all night and haven't caught anything. But because you say so, I will let down the nets." When they had done so, they caught such a large number of fish that their nets began to break. So they signaled their partners in the other boat to come and help them, and they came and filled both boats so full that they began to sink. When Simon Peter saw this, he fell at Jesus' knees and said, "Go away from me, Lord; I am a sinful man!" For he and all his companions were astonished at the catch of fish they had taken, and so were James and John, the sons of Zebedee, Simon's partners. Then Jesus said to Simon, "Don't be afraid; from now on you will fish for people." So they pulled their boats up on shore, left everything and followed him. (Luke 5: 4–11 NIV)

Acceptance

Disgraced by the disfigurement that defines who he is, the leper retreats to his shunned society. Here people of all ages suffer miserably from a topical disease that secretes contagious fluids from raised blisters swathed upon their tortured, nerve-damaged bodies. Isolated from family and friends, depression has manifested itself in the heart and mind of this desperate man. Within this tomb of misery, an inkling of hope arises as the sufferer believes in the healing powers of Jesus Christ. As he contemplates his options, he courageously decides to part from this secluded scene and search for the one who can save him. Boldly, he attempts to integrate with the attentive audience. Hoping that the elongated shawl will shield his identity, the leper winds his way to close proximity of the Master. Jesus' tender touch breaks the Levitical law and instantly cleanses him of the incurable ailment. Jesus cares for this leper who is ostracized by his own community. As we survey the power of Christ in this miraculous moment, let us not overlook the fact that He loves the unlovable. Instead of rejecting us because of our sin, Jesus acknowledges and cleanses us, setting us free from the bondage of our errant ways. Pursue Christ, for He is waiting to receive the flawed you.

A man with leprosy came to him and begged him on his knees, "If you are willing, you can make me clean." Jesus was indignant. He reached out his hand and touched the man. "I am willing," he said. "Be clean!" Immediately the leprosy left him and he was cleansed. (Mark 1:40–42 NIV)

Upheld

Jesus is home in Capernaum. A vast crowd is converging to witness His miracles and beliefs. Tightly compressed in the forum, sweat, heat, and breath merge to form unnerving conditions in this compact space. Jesus pauses and gazes upward as tiny particles of the roof begin to descend upon the unsuspecting audience. Daylight floods the darkened room as a rectangular opening materializes. The crowd quickly parts as four men lower a stretcher into their midst. Their paralyzed friend needs healing, and their strong faith has brought them squarely to the foot of Christ. The four men exert a fierce determination unencumbered by hindrances that might deter their ability to help a friend in need. When Jesus sees their faith, He says to the paralyzed man, "Son, your sins are forgiven." The faith of the four upholds their comrade, and he is exonerated and healed by the authority of Christ. Jesus then says to the man, "I tell you, get up, take your mat and go home." The restored man marches away, mercifully forgiven of sin and made well. Friends united in prayer will experience the power of Christ. Our Messiah can unlock the prison door of the mind and body and set us free. Come together, bow your heads, and discover the mighty hand of God who upholds you.

Jesus stepped into a boat, crossed over and came to his own town. Some men brought to him a paralyzed man, lying on a mat. When Jesus saw their faith, he said to the man, "Take heart, son; your sins are forgiven." (Matthew 9:1–2 NIV)

Immediately Jesus knew in his spirit that this was what they were thinking in their hearts, and he said to them, "Why are you thinking these things? Which is easier: to say to this paralyzed man, 'Your sins are forgiven,' or to say, 'Get up, take your mat and walk'? But I want you to know that the Son of Man has authority on earth to forgive sins." So he said to the man, "I tell you, get up, take your mat and go home." He got up, took his mat and walked out in full view of them all. This amazed everyone and they praised God, saying, "We have never seen anything like this!" (Mark 2: 8–12 NIV)

True Wealth

The heavy scent of fresh fish blends with the saltiness encrusted on his lips as the tax collector makes his way via the northern shore of the Sea of Galilee to his appointed customhouse. Daggered looks flash as he navigates a region of resentment. This is his home, but he feels like a stranger despised by his peers. For Matthew is a profitable publican who uses his lucrative position to extract funds from impoverished citizens struggling to make ends meet. Enduring excessive demands for their meager wages, they are forced to relinquish crucial earnings, subsidizing the Roman Empire. Matthew's contemporaries blame him for their dire predicament. In a strange God-ordained twist of fate, Matthew abruptly goes from serving money to serving the Lord. Jesus asks him to follow, and without hesitation he does. An educated writer and scribe, Matthew will one day record the detailed accounts of Christ's existence and breathe credibility throughout pages of Scripture. What would it be like to walk away from a storehouse of wealth that has been generated for years? To give up luxury for poverty? To go from succulent feasts to mere scraps of food? Matthew doesn't waver for he knows that spiritual wealth far exceeds material assets. Where does your treasure lie?

As Jesus went on from there, he saw a man named Matthew sitting at the tax collector's booth. "Follow me," he told him, and Matthew got up and followed him. (Matthew 9:9)

Miracles

Healing Waters

Five covered columns
parallel the Bethesda pool
where frothy moss lines
the edge of sparkling water.
Cascading droplets blow
gentle bubbles that swirl
and glide on a cool,
azure, liquid surface. The
hypnotic peacefulness
of the eddy quickly fades
as giggles, shrieks, and
jubilation saturate the air.
For this Sheep Gate pool
is a rumored site of healing.
Its occupants are the disabled:
blind, lame, and paralyzed who
have carried their frail bodies
and hopes to this place of
promise. Unable to dip himself
into the pool, an invalid lies
helpless on the uneven
sandstone ground. Surveying

his dire predicament, Jesus says
to him, "Pick up your mat and
walk." Elated, the cured man
saunters away. He has no idea
who his liberator is, for Jesus
has disappeared into the crowd.
This healing occurs on the
Sabbath, and it is at this
    junction
that Jesus begins to be persecuted
by the Jewish leaders for His
    "labor"
on a day of customized rest. Jesus'
response: "My Father is always at
His work, and I too am working."
Healing originates with faith, not
pools of water, and we can turn
to our Creator, even on the
    Sabbath,
with confidence that He cares for
us and will steadfastly sustain us
in every situation.

New International Version (NIV)

"Sir," the invalid replied, "I have no one to help me into the pool when the water is stirred. While I am trying to get in, someone else goes down ahead of me." Then Jesus said to him, "Get up! Pick up your mat and walk." At once the man was cured; he picked up his mat and walked. The day on which this took place was a Sabbath. (John 5:7–9 NIV)

Withered Hands

Crunching on the narrow path, the disciples carefully trod amidst the corn stalks ready for consumption. Ravenous, the tiny kernels look inviting and will suffice to ease hunger while renewing their sagging energy.

Plucking the heads of golden grain, the famished ones quickly ingest their simple meal. Ever vigilant, the Pharisees address Jesus. "Look! Your disciples are doing what is unlawful on the Sabbath." Clearly, man's rules often muddle the meaning of this ordained respite. Exercising His authority, Jesus responds, "'The Sabbath was made for man, not man for the Sabbath. So the Son of Man is Lord even of the Sabbath." As He ventures inside the synagogue, Christ surveys a man whose lowered head and flushed cheeks indicate humiliation in regard to his shriveled hand. "Stretch out your hand," Jesus commands, so he stretched it out, and it was completely restored. Looking for a reason to bring charges against Jesus, they ask Him, "Is it lawful to heal on the Sabbath?" Acts of compassion, tender deeds carried out in love, feats of kindness, all coupled with humility and selflessness, render themselves appropriate on the Sabbath. Like a withered hand, our capability is futile until we discover the restoring power of God's mercy and grace. The feeble hand becomes strong, and the good work of the Sabbath is accomplished.

New International Version (NIV)

At that time Jesus went through the grainfields on the Sabbath. His disciples were hungry and began to pick some heads of grain and eat them. When the Pharisees saw this, they said to him, "Look! Your disciples are doing what is unlawful on the Sabbath." (Matthew 12: 1–2 NIV)

Going on from that place, he went into their synagogue, and a man with a shriveled hand was there. Looking for a reason to bring charges against Jesus, they asked him, "Is it lawful to heal on the Sabbath?" He said to them, "If any of you has a sheep and it falls into a pit on the Sabbath, will you not take hold of it and lift it out? How much more valuable is a person than a sheep! Therefore it is lawful to do good on the Sabbath." Then he said to the man, "Stretch out your hand." So he stretched it out and it was completely restored, just as sound as the other. (Matthew 9–13 NIV)

Then he said to them, "The Sabbath was made for man, not man for the Sabbath. So the Son of Man is Lord even of the Sabbath." (Mark 2: 27–28 NIV)

Anonymity

Smothered within the throngs
of frantic people searching for
an end to their misery and
clinging to the promise of past
miracles, He understands their
immediate needs but longs for
peace. Clamoring for recognition,
the cries seem to escalate, and the
physical pushing and pulling on
His robe at times becomes intense.
Disease ridden, paraplegic, and
demon-possessed, they descend
upon Him with piercing shrieks
and incessant wailing. These
suffering individuals believe
Jesus is the answer to their
prayers. People from Judea,
Jerusalem, Idumea, and regions
across the Jordan flock to Jesus'
side. Pressed by the crowd, He
enters a small boat and escapes
the intimidating situation. Prayers
to His heavenly Father will provide
a sustaining power that flourishes
throughout His ministry. By unleashing
this power, Jesus is able to provide
restoration. Demons are exorcised

and, upon seeing Jesus, they fall
down in reverence and cry out,
"You are the Son of God." But He
gives them strict orders not to reveal
who He is. It would be easy for
Jesus to lavish in accolades and
notoriety, yet He chooses anonymity,
for His purpose on earth is to glorify
His father and save a sinful people.
He deserves every tribute, but
instead desires to do His Father's
work covertly. How do we serve our
Lord? Are our motives generated
by man's approval or recognition
or our pride? Call on Christ to provide
unpretentious love and authentic
compassion, for He is the cornerstone
of our faith: the distinctive, almighty Savior.

Jesus withdrew with his disciples to the lake, and a large crowd from
Galilee followed. When they heard about all he was doing, many
people came to him from Judea, Jerusalem, Idumea, and the regions
across the Jordan and around Tyre and Sidon. Because of the crowd
he told his disciples to have a small boat ready for him, to keep the
people from crowding him. For he had healed many, so that those
with diseases were pushing forward to touch him. Whenever the
impure spirits saw him, they fell down before him and cried out, "You
are the Son of God." But he gave them strict orders not to tell others
about him. (Mark 3:7–12 NIV)

Who Are We?

She had wandered for days, anxious to arrive at her appointed destination atop a hillside overlooking a serene, sparkling sea. Wildflowers blanket the terrain, and the air brushes softly against her cheek as she nestles atop a tiny perch that provides a clear view of the beautiful panorama. As the sun forms a murky haze that bakes her skin, she gazes upon this once-tranquil setting now inundated by the arrival of thousands who have come to absorb the wisdom of the renowned Jesus. Casting her attention on the gentle rabbi, it is hard to imagine that He has powers beyond their comprehension. Tales of miracles and resurrections have circulated among the spectators, who crave an opportunity to listen to the one they greatly revere. The words Jesus articulates in the Sermon on the Mount are transposed from the obvious, for the Lord speaks of blessings that reflect hardships such as being poor in spirit, mourning, meekness, and even being persecuted! How can these burdens be embraced as blessings? Their educator reminds them that their perception of self-image is grossly misconstrued. For Jesus wants us to know that what the world thinks of us and even how we view ourselves differs greatly from how God wants us to be. A pure heart, a peacemaker, one who seeks righteousness and loves his enemy; these are the traits paramount to our Creator. We are designed for His glory and His pleasure. Being true to God will allow us to be true to ourselves.

Blessed are the poor in spirit,
   for theirs is the kingdom of heaven.
Blessed are those who mourn,
   for they will be comforted.
Blessed are the meek,
   for they will inherit the earth.
Blessed are those who hunger and thirst for righteousness,
   for they will be filled.
Blessed are the merciful,
   for they will be shown mercy.
Blessed are the pure in heart,
   for they will see God.
Blessed are the peacemakers,
   for they will be called children of God.
Blessed are those who are persecuted because of righteousness,
   for theirs is the kingdom of heaven. (Matthew 5:3–10 NIV)

Swap of Authority

The royal official seeks the favor of a lowly carpenter. Imagine this spectacle and the talk among the townsfolk! How could the centurion stoop to such a level to save the life of his servant? The bureaucrat favors this man who has devoted his life to serving his master. Efforts to revive his health have failed and alas, he is near death. Jesus' healing reputation offers hope and, representing him, Jewish friends offer a plea for restoration. On the winding path leading to the home, the centurion's friend approaches Jesus and offers an explanation on his behalf. "Lord, don't trouble yourself, for I do not deserve to have you come under my roof. That is why I did not even consider myself worthy to come to you. But say the word, and my servant will be healed. For I myself am a man under authority, with soldiers under me." Astonished, Jesus responds to the crowd, "I tell you, I have not found such great faith even in Israel." Instantly the servant is healed. When we approach God with genuine penitence, respect His authority, and acknowledge that He is our Lord, our faith will surge in humble appreciation.

For I myself am a man under authority, with soldiers under me. I tell this one, 'Go,' and he goes; and that one, 'Come,' and he comes. I say to my servant, 'Do this,' and he does it."

When Jesus heard this, he was amazed at him, and turning to the crowd following him, he said, "I tell you, I have not found such great faith even in Israel." Then the men who had been sent returned to the house and found the servant well. (Luke 7: 8–10 NIV)

Beheld

The small wooden
stretcher is draped
in a pale linen cloth
and transported by
pallbearers down the
grimy, mud-packed
road of Nain toward
the church. Wailing cries,
anguished sobs, and
chants reverberate
as the parade grieves
the death of a widow's
son. Jesus crosses the
path of this spectacle
and sees the boy's
mother. Although she
is greatly suffering, she
does not cry out for help
or ask Jesus for a miracle.
Compassion swells as
He recognizes her vast
sorrow. Moreover, He
personally feels her pain.
In response Jesus says,
"Young man, I say
to you, get up." The dead
boy sits up and begins to
talk, and Jesus gives him
back to his mother.
Our precious Savior
suffered unimaginable
affliction, and as a result,
He empathizes with our
misery. How reassuring
to know that no matter
the circumstance we
can turn to Him, because
we are His to behold.

Then he went up and touched the bier they were carrying him on, and the bearers stood still. He said, "Young man, I say to you, get up!" The dead man sat up and began to talk, and Jesus gave him back to his mother. (Luke 7:14–15 NIV)

Cascade

Jesus enters the elaborate
home of Simon the Pharisee.
Ornate furnishings occupy the
lavish complex of this wealthy
man. Reclining on a couch, feet
stretched out, Jesus
begins to engage in conversation
with His dining companions. The
enticing scents of bread and
succulent lamb drift through the
air. Abruptly, the door flies open,
and a known prostitute advances
carrying a lovely, intricately fashioned
alabaster jar. "As she stood behind
Jesus at His feet weeping, she began to
wet His feet with her tears. Then she
wiped them with her hair, kissed them
and poured perfume on them." Cascades
of tears, expensive perfume, and love
anoint her beloved Jesus. Shunned by
the spectators, her only focus is on her
precious Savior. Outraged and embarrassed
by the interruption, Simon's reaction is
met with a rebuke, for Jesus compares
the adoration of this scandalous woman to
the lack of respect shown to Him by His host.

"Then Jesus said to her, Your sins are forgiven.
Your faith has saved you; go in peace." Free
from the bondage of sin, she is able to go forth
and live a life secure in the mercy and favor
of a Father who loves her unconditionally.
Pour out your heart upon the One who loves
you dearly, precious one, for mercy awaits
those who seek forgiveness, regardless of the
sin. Let Him cascade His grace upon you.

Then he turned toward the woman and said to Simon, "Do you
see this woman? I came into your house. You did not give me any
water for my feet, but she wet my feet with her tears and wiped
them with her hair. You did not give me a kiss, but this woman,
from the time I entered, has not stopped kissing my feet. You did
not put oil on my head, but she has poured perfume on my feet.
Therefore, I tell you, her many sins have been forgiven—as her great
love has shown. But whoever has been forgiven little loves little."
Then Jesus said to her, "Your sins are forgiven." The other guests
began to say among themselves, "Who is this who even forgives
sins?" Jesus said to the woman, "Your faith has saved you; go in peace."
(Luke 7:44–50 NIV)

Family

The crowd multiplies and presses
against Jesus while attentively
concentrating on His every word.
Outside the structure His family waits
eagerly to speak to Him. James, Judas,
Simon, Joseph, and His two sisters
have accompanied their mother,
Mary, to impart their concern about
the direction of Jesus' ministry.
Having grown up with Jesus, the
family is familiar with the private
aspects of His life. Together they
share a sense of personal history:
family values, dutiful chores and
responsibilities, humorous stories,
practical jokes, and common life
experiences. They understand each
other's strengths and weaknesses
and feel comfortable exchanging
opinions as well as reprimands
when warranted. And now
they feel justified to do so for
the "sake of the family." At this
point the siblings do not believe
Jesus' rhetoric but some, mercifully,
change their opinion in due time.

Mary understands Jesus' divinity
and purpose but, she yearns
to protect her beloved son from
harm. Their request for an exclusive
appointment is denied, and Jesus
rebukes them. "Who is my mother, and
who are my brothers?" Pointing to His
disciples, He said, "Here are my mother
and my brothers. For whoever does
the will of my Father in heaven is my
brother and sister and mother." Hurt
and humiliated, they turn away from
the loved one who is no longer
their own. The family's place should
have been beside Jesus, listening, learning,
and gleaning wisdom rather than standing
aloof demanding His attention. The concerns
of our soul are a priority over the matters
of this world. You are Jesus' spiritual
family; now and forever cling to Him.

While Jesus was still talking to the crowd, his mother and
brothers stood outside, wanting to speak to him. Someone told him,
"Your mother and brothers are standing outside, wanting to speak
to you." He replied to him, "Who is my mother, and who are my
brothers?" (Matthew 12:46–48 NIV)

Storm at Sea

A thunderous clap erupts
as a slice of light illuminates
the tiny fishing vessel.
Fierce winds toss
the boat to and fro
amid the intense rhythm
of prevailing waves.
Swirling crests crash
over planks, drenching
the huddled inhabitants.
The inky darkness swallows
up the sodden craft, and the
bright stars are replaced by
gray clouds infiltrating the sky.
Terrified and certain of
    impending death,
Jesus' disciples scream
as they plead for help.

In the pandemonium,
Jesus slumbers soundly.
Sleep deprived and
fatigued, He has finally
been lulled asleep by
the hypnotizing motion
of the lilting waves.
Jarred awake by the
commotion, His reaction
confuses His companions.
Calmly Jesus raises His
hands, and the turbulent
sea is immediately at rest.
In the hushed stillness, the
enthralled spectators
discover that inner peace
originates with one source,
Christ, our Sovereign King.

He replied, "You of little faith, why are you so afraid?" Then he got
up and rebuked the winds and the waves, and it was completely calm.
(Matthew 8:26 NIV)

Legion

Dank tunnels form a maze
leading to the mausoleums
that house the deceased
in the bowels of the
region of Gerasenes.
Tormented for years,
ostracized from his
loved ones, an
anguished soul
races in the
isolated corridors
screaming, clawing
at his face, and cutting
himself with stones.
Previously captured
and shackled, Legion's
abundant strength
breaks the chains, and
the elusive captive
cannot be restrained.
Frantically, he emerges
into the light of day and
falls on his knees
as he confronts Jesus,
who is exiting His boat.
Shouting, he proclaims,

"What do you want with
me, Jesus, Son of the Most
High God? In God's name
don't torture me!" For
Jesus had said to him,
"Come out of this man,
you impure spirit!" Then
the numerous demons exit
his angst-ridden body and
enter the two thousand swine
feeding on a hillside. Dashing
   down
the precipitous bank, they drown
in the lake, freeing Legion at last.
In order to reach this plagued
individual, Jesus has battled a
   storm
on the sea and rowed seven and
one half miles to the region. This
madman is just one of many
who reside in this place of
solitude and detachment.
Jesus is willing to go to any
   length
to meet you in any place—
regardless of your regretful

choices or circumstances— when you open your heart to Him. Christ instructs the placid man, "Go home to your own people and tell them how much the Lord has done for you, and how He has had mercy on you." Discover that true restoration is found only in Christ.

When he saw Jesus from a distance, he ran and fell on his knees in front of him. He shouted at the top of his voice, "What do you want with me, Jesus, Son of the Most High God? In God's name don't torture me!" For Jesus had said to him, "Come out of this man, you impure spirit!" Then Jesus asked him, "What is your name?" "My name is Legion," he replied, "for we are many." And he begged Jesus again and again not to send them out of the area. A large herd of pigs was feeding on the nearby hillside. The demons begged Jesus, "Send us among the pigs; allow us to go into them." He gave them permission, and the impure spirits came out and went into the pigs. The herd, about two thousand in number, rushed down the steep bank into the lake and were drowned. (Mark 5: 13 NIV)

Asleep

Many fathers would have
   mourned
their loss and melted into
   despair,
but not this one. The synagogue
   ruler,
mighty in power and wealth,
   knows
that there is only one option:
   Jesus.
Confident that Christ's hand will
reinstate the life of his precious
daughter, he seeks out the one
who offers hope to the dejected.
Jesus agrees to travel to the
   believer's
home to revive the lifeless child.
Upon entering the darkened
   room,
muffled cries and wails can be
   heard as
mourners grieve the loss of this
precious young girl. Bending at
her side, Jesus' compassionate
eyes survey the lamentation and
   ridicule,
as well as the hope resonating
in her anxious parent.
Taking the hand of the "sleeping"
girl, she awakens, and a
joyful celebration takes place.
Her father's deep faith has
ensured miraculous results.
While we passively participate
in our faith walk, we can miss
many opportunities to impact
God's kingdom. We need to
"wake up" and actively move
according to His will, thus
living out the glorious plan
and potential He has created
for our existence. Rise and shine!

When Jesus entered the synagogue leader's house and saw the noisy crowd and people playing pipes, he said, "Go away. The girl is not dead but asleep." But they laughed at him. After the crowd had been put outside, he went in and took the girl by the hand, and she got up. News of this spread through all that region. (Matthew 9:23–26 NIV)

Touch

Twelve horrific years of bleeding,
searching for answers, coming up short.
Fruitless efforts by countless physicians and
failed treatments and remedies have
now resulted in desperation. Hearing
of the healing powers of Jesus, she
has a renewed sense of hope as
she traverses the beaten path
into the city where He is preaching.
Slithering through the dense crowd,
she aggressively makes her way
toward the proximity of His presence.
Hands trembling, she reaches out to
touch His faded linen cloak, "because
she thought, 'If I just touch His clothes,
I will be healed.' Immediately her
bleeding stops and she feels in her
body that she is freed from her suffering."
The authoritative power of Christ can
restore your physical, mental, and spiritual
anguish. You need to seek Him first, not
last, for He knows the intricate details
of your mind, body, and soul. Jesus wants
you to reach out to Him so He can touch
you with His healing powers. As the
woman lay at Christ's feet, tears

flowing with gratitude, He said,
"Daughter, your faith has healed you.
Go in peace and be freed from your suffering."
A sense of tranquility is attainable as you
release yourself to the one and only
physician who adeptly medicates with love.

When she heard about Jesus, she came up behind him in the crowd and touched his cloak, because she thought, "If I just touch his clothes, I will be healed." Immediately her bleeding stopped and she felt in her body that she was freed from her suffering. At once Jesus realized that power had gone out from him. He turned around in the crowd and asked, "Who touched my clothes?" "You see the people crowding against you," his disciples answered, "and yet you can ask, 'Who touched me?'" (Mark 5:27–30 NIV)

Persistence

Bursting through the door of the house where Jesus is lodging, the two blind men stumble and frantically call out, "Have mercy on us, son of David!" Having fumbled, tripped, and searched the streets for their champion, they exuberantly clamber into His presence. For these devotés believe Jesus to be the Messiah and readily proclaim that conviction throughout the streets of Capernaum. Testing their commitment, Jesus momentarily hesitates in fulfilling their request and then questions, "Do you believe that I am able to do this?" Unrelentingly they cry out a resounding, "Yes, Lord." Gently touching their eyes, He assures them, "According to your faith let it be done to you,"

and their sight is restored. Steadfast devotion consists of prayer, patience, and persistence. Release yourself completely to the healer of your mind, body, and soul.

As Jesus went on from there, two blind men followed him, calling out, "Have mercy on us, Son of David!" When he had gone indoors, the blind men came to him, and he asked them, "Do you believe that I am able to do this?" "Yes, Lord," they replied. Then he touched their eyes and said, "According to your faith let it be done to you"; and their sight was restored. Jesus warned them sternly, "See that no one knows about this." But they went out and spread the news about him all over that region. (Matthew 9:27–31 NIV)

Unresponsive

The comfort of familiarity inhabits His
thoughts as Jesus once again travels
the road that leads to His hometown.
Observing the familiar buildings,
paths, and groves of trees where
He played as a youth, His eyes mist
with the longing and love of adored
family and friends. He hopes this
reunion will differ from the previous
one when He was ostracized and
fled for safety. However, Jesus wants to
offer His comrades another chance at
redemption so He bravely enters
the synagogue during the Sabbath and
begins to teach and perform miracles.
Word of His return initiates a crowd
of protesters, and the heckling begins.
Offended by His suggested divine
authority, they accuse Jesus of
hypocrisy and deceitfulness. His peers
believe Him to be a simple carpenter,
a son of Mary and Joseph, a nice
boy from the neighborhood, and
one who is certainly void of special
powers and heavenly knowledge.
Sadly recognizing the hindrance to His

effectiveness, Jesus says to them, "A prophet is not without honor except in his own town, among his relatives and in his own home." Thus few miracles occurred in Nazareth, and Jesus left to seek those who would respond to God's truth. We, like Jesus, do not have to be respected or honored to serve our God. Don't let rejection prevent you from completing your mission. It is only His approval that matters.

Coming to his hometown, he began teaching the people in their synagogue, and they were amazed. "Where did this man get this wisdom and these miraculous powers?" they asked. Isn't this the carpenter's son? Isn't his mother's name Mary, and aren't his brothers James, Joseph, Simon and Judas? Aren't all his sisters with us? Where then did this man get all these things?" And they took offense at him. But Jesus said to them, "A prophet is not without honor except in his own town and in his own home." And he did not do many miracles there because of their lack of faith. (Matthew 13:54–58 NIV)

Share

The time has come. Jesus has been preparing the twelve for this moment. Birds chirp, a soft breeze rustles the trees, and the solitude of this garden will soon dissipate as the enthusiastic disciples are summoned. Equipped with the shield of faith and the sword of Scripture, they are ready for the next phase of their discipleship: active ministry. Jesus' emotions vary from exhilaration for their purpose to anxiety for their safety. He knows what this ministry will cost each one, but the work needs to be done, and these are the chosen. By "giving them authority to drive out impure spirits and to heal every disease and sickness," these faithful will carry God with them as they execute His plan.

Christ's final instructions are specific and cautionary. He understands their human frailties and the consequences of impulsive behavior. "Go to the lost sheep of Israel. As you go, proclaim this message: 'The kingdom of heaven has come near.' Heal the sick, raise the dead, cleanse those who have leprosy, drive out demons. Freely you have received; freely give." As we venture into our ministry for Christ, we are reminded that we have done nothing to receive our salvation. God has freely given us this gift. We are to share this good news with a lost world searching for God's light. Mightily equipped with our faith, scripture, and prayer, we are prepared for this daunting venture. Go and freely give of yourself in our blessed Jesus' name.

Jesus called his twelve disciples to him and gave them authority to drive out impure spirits and to heal every disease and sickness. (Matthew 10:1 NIV)

These twelve Jesus sent out with the following instructions: "Do not go among the Gentiles or enter any town of the Samaritans. Go rather to the lost sheep of Israel. As you go, proclaim this message: 'The kingdom of heaven has come near.' Heal the sick, raise the dead, cleanse those who have leprosy, drive out demons. Freely you have received; freely give." (Matthew 10:5–8 NIV)

Enough

The golden sun drips
its final rays upon
a captive audience.
A tangerine haze
splashes the horizon as
the solar descent begins.
Restlessly seated near his
protective mother, the
boy gazes upward and
instantly receives an
approving smile and a
tender embrace. Wisely,
she has come prepared with
provisions, anticipating an
extensive, mesmerizing event.
Inspired by Jesus' stories,
passion, and love, the
lad's need to respond
surges. Impulsively, he
grabs the woven basket
that cradles five barley
loaves and two small fish.
Skipping past the famished
and weary crowd, he proudly
presents his treasure to the
disciple Andrew. After
blessing this generous gift,
Jesus distributes the meager
meal, which miraculously
satisfies five thousand
    spectators.
When we fully give ourselves
to Christ it is always enough.
For He uses our unselfish gift to
broaden His mighty kingdom.
This truly is the gift
that keeps on giving.

Here is a boy with five small barley loaves and two small fish, but how
far will they go among so many?" (John 6:9 NIV)

Little Faith

The lake's solace is beckoning;
the destination is Gennesaret.
Clambering aboard the wobbly
vessel, the disciples venture forth
while notably absent is their
mentor, teacher, and friend, Jesus.
The fierce wind blocks the passage
causing a gradual progression.
The sun dips into the horizon,
with blinking stars
appearing in the thickening sky.
During the fourth watch of the night,
a sinewy figure appears to be
floating atop the waves cradling
the jarring craft. Luminous, the
silhouette seems to be an
apparition. In the wailing
roar of the wind, Jesus' reassuring
voice cascades upon the frightened
assembly as He eases the escalating
trepidation in their hearts.
Impulsively, Peter leaps over
the starboard side and marches
on the water, never wavering as
his eyes fixate upon those of
his precious Lord. Alas, distracted

by the sting of the hammering wind,
his sight shifts to the mass buoying
his body, and he begins to submerge.
Pitifully, he resorts to cries of help.
As Jesus grasps his trembling hand,
He rebukes him saying, "You
of little faith, why did you doubt?"
Abundant faith materializes in those
who steadfastly turn to Jesus Christ.

Shortly before dawn Jesus went out to them, walking on the lake. When the disciples saw him walking on the lake, they were terrified. "It's a ghost," they said, and cried out in fear. But Jesus immediately said to them: "Take courage! It is I. Don't be afraid." "Lord, if it's you," Peter replied, "tell me to come to you on the water." "Come," he said. Then Peter got down out of the boat, walked on the water and came toward Jesus. But when he saw the wind, he was afraid and, beginning to sink, cried out, "Lord, save me!" Immediately Jesus reached out his hand and caught him. "You of little faith," he said, "why did you doubt?" And when they climbed into the boat, the wind died down. (Matthew 14:25–32 NIV)

Bread

Tentatively, the little boy tears off a morsel of the warm, toasty bread. Starving, he guards the impulse to seize the entire slice and gobble it, but he knows that others in his family are hungry and this soft delicacy must be shared. Jesus said, "I am the bread of life, he who comes to me will never go hungry, and he who believes in me will never be thirsty." Famished for spiritual nourishment, we often find ourselves attempting to meet our needs through materialistic alternatives. Although temporarily pleasing, they fail to gratify our God-seeking soul. The iconic image of bread is reverently used as a Communion element. The consumption of bread and wine further symbolizes the triumph of life over death because of our Savior's tremendous sacrifice. Take and eat, for there is plenty to go around. The bread of life awaits you, and Jesus will satisfy you with the feast of the Holy Spirit.

Then Jesus declared, "I am the bread of life. Whoever comes to me will never go hungry, and whoever believes in me will never be thirsty. (John 6:35 NIV)

Harvest

The gentle breeze
rustles the golden
stalks basking
in the brilliant sunshine.
Swaying to and fro,
they appear to dance
while the stifled crackle
serves as a symphonic,
orchestral performance.
Tiny granules begin
to form at the tips of
these slender fingers.
Soon the yield will provide
bountiful nourishment.
Jesus equates this spectacle
with the ripe harvest field
of God. The cultivation of
wheat symbolizes the mass
of humanity in need of
a Savior. People everywhere
are overwhelmed by daily
strife, illness, misery, and
despair. Hope is found
in our Deliverer. Our loving
teacher explains, "The harvest
is plentiful. It is ripe enough
to be gathered into the barns."
The laborers, you and I, are
few in number to reap the
crop. Jesus has pressed His love
and compassion for others
onto our souls, and united
we need to enter the field and
stockpile the precious resource.
As we reach out to others, the
love of God filters throughout
a world in need of salvation.

Jesus went through all the towns and villages, teaching in their synagogues, proclaiming the good news of the kingdom and healing every disease and sickness. When he saw the crowds, he had compassion on them, because they were harassed and helpless, like sheep without a shepherd. Then he said to his disciples, "The harvest is plentiful but the workers are few. Ask the Lord of the harvest, therefore, to send out workers into his harvest field." (Matthew 9:35–38 NIV)

Steadfast Faith

Broken slabs of stone mark the main street of Tyre. Surrounded by a crowd as He ventures through the city, Jesus pauses to minister to the throng. A Canaanite woman's pleading voice pierces the dialogue and grows increasingly irritating as Christ ignores her continuous petitions. Tears stream as she begs for Jesus to heal her demon-possessed daughter. Disregarding her request, Jesus turns and walks away from the pitiful mother. Unrelenting, she follows Him, sobbing and beseeching Him for help. The disciples, annoyed with her tantrums, ask Jesus to send her away. He responds, "It is not right to take the children's bread and toss it to the dogs." Kneeling, she implores, "Even the dogs eat the crumbs that fall from their Master's table." Recognizing her remarkable faith in her reverent and humble response, Jesus immediately restores her daughter's physical state. As we pray to God, remember this example of perseverance and resolve flanked by tremendous faith that ultimately impacts God's answer to our petition. Jesus recognizes and honors our devotion as we relentlessly pursue our loving Master.

A Canaanite woman from that vicinity came to him, crying out, "Lord, Son of David, have mercy on me! My daughter is demon-possessed and suffering terribly." Jesus did not answer a word. So his disciples came to him and urged him, "Send her away, for she keeps crying out after us." He answered, "I was sent only to the lost sheep of Israel." The woman came and knelt before him. "Lord, help me!" she said. He replied, "It is not right to take the children's bread and toss it to the dogs." "Yes it is, Lord," she said. "Even the dogs eat the crumbs that fall from their master's table." Then Jesus said to her, "Woman, you have great faith! Your request is granted." And her daughter was healed at that moment. (Matthew 15: 22–28 NIV)

Impart

Silence, solitude, and suffering
are encapsulated in a world void
of communication and interaction.
The deaf-mute man's companions
are compelled to bring him to
the one who can alleviate the
barriers that eradicate the joy
of fellowship for this pitiful soul.
Traveling in predominately
Jewish communities, Jesus now
steps into the confines of Decapolis
and finds Himself in
a colony of ten cities linked together
with an open temple where imperial
cults worship the renowned Roman
emperor. Having traveled upon Roman
roads that crisscross multiple
temples and imposing public structures,
the Gentiles full of expectations
of healing and inspiration seek the
wondrous Jewish rabbi. Here the
impaired man arrives at the
Savior's feet and his friends beg
for restoration. In privacy, Jesus
"places His fingers in the man's ears.
Then He spit and touches the man's

tongue. Looking up to heaven He
says, 'Ephphatha' (be opened). At
this, the man's ears are opened, his
tongue is loosened and he begins
to speak plainly." The Lord bestows
His power, and the physical shackles
shatter, setting this prisoner free.
As we open our eyes, ears, and heart
to Christ, He imparts mercy and grace,
thus enabling us to go forth basking
in His almighty love and forgiveness.

He looked up to heaven and with a deep sigh said to him, " (which
means "Be opened!"). At this, the man's ears were opened, his tongue
was loosened and he began to speak plainly. Jesus commanded them
not to tell anyone. But the more he did so, the more they kept talking
about it. People were overwhelmed with amazement. "He has done
everything well," they said. "He even makes the deaf hear and the
mute speak." (Mark 7:34–37 NIV)

Liberated

Clutched within the grip of evil,
Mary of Magdala suffers greatly.
Seven demonic spirits haunt her
body and have caused
   immeasurable
damage to herself as well as the
relationships she has cultivated.
Malevolent actions, words, and
decisions have resulted from a
terrible origin in her tortured
   mind.
In retrospect, she despises the
person she has become; however,
her ability to squash the
wickedness is fruitless. Mary
desires to have a peaceful
and loving mindset that
embraces the company
of others, tends to their
needs, and offers love.
In desperation, she places
her hope in Jesus. Mary
has faith that Jesus will
restore her soul. Uttering
His words of power, the
demons immediately flee from
Mary's body, never to return.
Liberated from this inward
prison, Mary discovers a
world foreign to her own.
Happiness, fulfillment, love,
kindness, and compassion
are now potentially attainable.
Her benevolent Lord has granted
her grace and restoration. From
that moment on, Mary of
   Magdala
became one of Jesus' most ardent
followers. We too can be delivered
from our yoke of sin through
repentance and consequently
the merciful love of Christ.

After this, Jesus traveled about from one town and village to another, proclaiming the good news of the kingdom of God. The Twelve were with him, and also some women who had been cured of evil spirits and diseases: Mary (called Magdalene) from whom seven demons had come out. (Luke 8:1–2 NIV)

Provision

The lull of the boat's sway cannot
soothe the apprehension of its crew.
The hour is late and the disciples are
famished. Preoccupied with the day's
events, they have forgotten to bring
provisions. Blaming one another,
the intensified emotions lead to
heated complaints about the sole
loaf of bread they had that would
need to suffice.
Hearing the squabbles, Jesus
cautions, "Be careful. Watch out for
the yeast of the Pharisees and that of
Herod." Confused, they respond, "It
is because we have no bread." Jesus
asks them, "Why are you talking about
having no bread? Do you still not see
or understand? Are your hearts hardened?
Do you have eyes but fail to see me, and
ears but fail to hear? And don't you
remember?" Twice the Messiah has
furnished meals for thousands with
little more than a few loaves of bread,
and now the witnesses to these
miracles are questioning His care.
When we depend on each other

instead of God, we place ourselves
in harm's way. Just as yeast rapidly
ferments and reproduces, so can evil
as it proliferates through the arrogant
actions of man in society. Conversely,
reliance on God results in complete
satisfaction—physically, mentally, and
spiritually. Remember Christ's response
to your past tribulations and place
Him squarely in charge of your future.

The disciples had forgotten to bring bread, except for one loaf they
had with them in the boat. "Be careful," Jesus warned them. "Watch
out for the yeast of the Pharisees and that of Herod." They discussed
this with one another and said, "It is because we have no bread." Aware
of their discussion, Jesus asked them: "Why are you talking about
having no bread? Do you still not see or understand? Are your
hearts hardened? Do you have eyes but fail to see, and ears but fail
to hear? And don't you remember? When I broke the five loaves for
the five thousand, how many basketfuls of pieces did you pick up?"
"Twelve," they replied. "And when I broke the seven loaves for the
four thousand, how many basketfuls of pieces did you pick up?" They
answered, "Seven." He said to them, "Do you still not understand?"
(Mark 8: 14–21 NIV)

Teaching

Identify

Porous moss clings to the trunk of a statuesque olive tree providing shade for the clustered disciples and their mentor in the emerald Caesarea grove. Deep in discussion, Jesus suddenly asks, "Who do the people say the Son of Man is?" Equating Him with John the Baptist and Elijah, the disciples struggle to articulate the exalted significance of their adored leader. Simon Peter eagerly responds, "You are the Christ, the Son of the living God." Jesus then blesses Peter, for this realization was "not revealed to him by man, but by my Father in Heaven." Our faith has to be a personal matter. Knowledge alone will not bring us to our knees. In order to truly know our Savior, we must delve into our spiritual bank. Vulnerability, trust, repentance, and blind faith guide us to the heart of God. Ask yourself today: Who is Jesus Christ to you?

"But what about you?" he asked. "Who do you say I am?" Simon Peter answered, "You are the Messiah, the Son of the living God." (Matthew 16:15–16 NIV)

Transformation

The three disciples amble up the
steep incline of the mountain trailing
behind their mentor and friend, Jesus.
Curious as to why they have been
chosen, the trio anxiously anticipates
what might await them at the summit.
Resting at the peak, Peter, James, and
John bow their heads and earnestly pray.
Glancing up, they are astonished to see
Jesus' face begins to transform. The dazzling
brightness penetrates their vision. In addition,
His clothes radiate a vivid whiteness that
appears as a flash of light transparent
in nature. "Two men, Moses and Elijah,
appear in glorious splendor, talking
with Jesus. They speak about His departure
which He is about to bring to fulfillment
at Jerusalem." Besieged by the splendor,
Peter desires to signify the event by
erecting three shelters. However, while he is
rambling, an incandescent cloud envelops
the assembly and a resolved voice states,
"This is my Son, whom I have chosen; listen
to Him." We do not need shelters to commune
with our Savior, for He is beside us always.
God wants to reveal Himself to us. The more

we want to receive, the more He is willing to share. The reality of Christ is so much more than we can ever imagine! Ask God to modify your perception of Him, and open your mind to the mystery and wonder of our glorious and almighty Creator.

About eight days after Jesus said this, he took Peter, John and James with him and went up onto a mountain to pray. As he was praying, the appearance of his face changed, and his clothes became as bright as a flash of lightning. Two men, Moses and Elijah, appeared in glorious splendor, talking with Jesus. They spoke about his departure, which he was about to bring to fulfillment at Jerusalem. (Luke 9:28–31 NIV)

Seeds of Faith

The disciples felt helpless.
Their efforts to remove the
demon from the boy were in
    vain.
Convulsing from seizures, eyes
rolled back, arms flailing, the
suffering had taken its toll.
Tossing himself into fire and
    water, the
possessed child's self-inflicted
pain is becoming perilous.
Breaking through the throng,
his agitated father pleads with
Jesus to make his son whole.
Frustrated with the crowd's
lack of belief, our rabbi's anger
simmers as He reprimands the
demon, and the boy is healed.
Later, the disappointed chosen
twelve ask Christ why they
had been unsuccessful.
Resolutely He responds,
"Because you have so little faith.
Truly I tell you, if you have faith
as small as a mustard seed, you
can say to this mountain,
'Move from here to there,' and
it will move. Nothing will be
impossible for you." Picture
a tiny seed and imagine the
power of faith you hold in
your hand. How big is your
God? Do you believe He can
make a mountain move with
a single command, or have you
placed Him in a box in which
He has human limitations?
Open your mind and heart
to the unsurpassable power
of your Lord and believe.

When they came to the crowd, a man approached Jesus and knelt before him. "Lord, have mercy on my son," he said. "He has seizures and is suffering greatly. He often falls into the fire or into the water. I brought him to your disciples, but they could not heal him." "You unbelieving and perverse generation," Jesus replied, "how long shall I stay with you? How long shall I put up with you? Bring the boy here to me." Jesus rebuked the demon, and it came out of the boy, and he was healed at that moment. Then the disciples came to Jesus in private and asked, "Why couldn't we drive it out?" He replied, "Because you have so little faith. Truly I tell you, if you have faith as small as a mustard seed, you can say to this mountain, 'Move from here to there,' and it will move. Nothing will be impossible for you." (Matthew 17: 14–20 NIV)

Reality Check

They had heard it before, and they did
not want to hear it again. After all, it is
another beautiful day in Galilee, and all
this talk of dying is making them miserable.
Why does Jesus continue to talk about His
death? After all, He is the son of God and
surely His Father will not allow that dire
fate to happen? "Listen carefully to what
I am about to tell you: The Son of Man is
going to be delivered into the hands of men."
They speculate, "How can this possibly
occur?" The disciples themselves are
eyewitnesses to countless miracles, and it
appears obvious that nothing can prevent
Jesus from achieving success. Our Savior
knows His time of suffering is near, and He
wants His beloved friends to gain the
wisdom needed to carry on after He returns
to heaven, but He is frustrated with their
apathetic response. Sadly, the message of
hope locked in the resurrection is also
overlooked and will not be comprehended
until Pentecost. "They will kill Him, and after
three days He will rise." But they did not
understand what this meant. It was hidden
from them, so they did not grasp it and

"they were afraid to ask Him about it." Focused
on their fabricated plans for Jesus, they
chose to believe that He is an earthly king
assembling a political kingdom where each one
of them will have an important role. If Jesus is
slain then all hope of this bright future is
obliterated. Jesus plainly teaches us the truth, and
we can either accept it and move forward or remain
ignorant, ashamed to ask questions, thereby
thwarting the opportunity to fully serve Him better.
Let's stop for a reality check: Are we in tune with
Christ's plan or our own? Open your eyes to the
truth and trust Him with the providential outcome.

They left that place and passed through Galilee. Jesus did not
want anyone to know where they were, because he was teaching his
disciples. He said to them, "The Son of Man is going to be delivered
into the hands of men. They will kill him, and after three days he
will rise." But they did not understand what he meant and were afraid
to ask him about it. (Mark 9:30–32 NIV)

Tax Exemption

The rickety wooden frame of the tax collector's table serves as a depository for the temple preservation taxes in Capernaum. Approaching the disciple Peter, the collectors question him:

"Doesn't your teacher pay the temple tax?' Peter readily agrees, for each Jewish male is required to pay two-drachma. Before a word is spoken, Jesus immediately determines what is on Peter's mind. "From whom do the kings of the earth collect duty and taxes—from their own children or from others?" "From others," Peter answers. "Then the children are exempt," replies Jesus.

Jesus perceives our thoughts even before they are spoken. His kingly role will be revealed through a miracle that verifies His power over poverty. Obeying a directive from Jesus, Simon Peter casts his line and ensnares a fish with four drachma coins lodged in its mouth.

Rather than offending, compliance in payment is made, but the source is proven to originate with God. Through our obedience as well as involvement, God will supply exactly what we require. For Christ is the supreme ruler and we are his children.

After Jesus and his disciples arrived in Capernaum, the collectors of the two-drachma temple tax came to Peter and asked, "Doesn't your teacher pay the temple tax?" "Yes, he does," he replied. When Peter came into the house, Jesus was the first to speak. "What do you think, Simon?" he asked. "From whom do the kings of the earth collect duty and taxes—from their own children or from others?" "From others," Peter answered. "Then the children are exempt," Jesus said to him. "But so that we may not cause offense, go to the lake and throw out your line. Take the first fish you catch; open its mouth and you will find a four-drachma coin. Take it and give it to them for my tax and yours." (Matthew 17:24–27 NIV)

Childlike Spirit

Walking along the hot, dusty road
to Capernaum, the disciples' friendly
banter soon turns argumentative.
Three had witnessed the transfiguration,
and a select few had observed Christ's miracles,
resulting in an atmosphere of superiority.
Egotistical attitudes flare into tempers as
angry shouts are exchanged for the
remainder of the journey. "Jesus, knowing
their thoughts, takes a little child and has him
stand beside Him. Then He says to them,
"Whoever welcomes this little child in my
name welcomes me; and whoever welcomes
me welcomes the one who sent me. For it is
the one who is least among you all who is the
greatest." The pliability of a child is reflected
in his trusting nature, eagerness to learn,
dependency on parental authority, and
willingness to obey. A child's innocence, joyful
disposition, affection, and kindness reveal
a spiritual temperament. Pride barricades
the channel of love Christ flows though us to
others. In essence, Jesus taught that the least
among us will be the greatest in heaven. An
unpretentious manner, complete with a heart
of acceptance and love, jointly create Christlike

greatness in a sea of humanity that often credits
monetary worth and leadership strength as success.
Today, humbly present yourself to God and ask Him
to "create a pure heart, and renew your steadfast spirit."

An argument started among the disciples as to which of them would
be the greatest. Jesus, knowing their thoughts, took a little child and
had him stand beside him. Then he said to them, "Whoever welcomes
this little child in my name welcomes me; and whoever welcomes me
welcomes the one who sent me. For it is the one who is least among
you all who is the greatest." (Luke 9:46–48 NIV)

Create in me a pure heart, O God, and renew a steadfast spirit within
me. (Psalm 51:10 NIV)

Reaction

Jesus, the Son of God, is the
target for an assassination.
Warned to stay away from the
Feast of Tabernacles, He ignores
the advice and stealthily enters the
celebration commemorating the
Israelites' journey through the desert.
Interwoven in the crowd, Jewish
leaders survey the spectators
anticipating Jesus' arrival. Halfway
through the festivities, Christ boldly
emerges in the temple courtyard
and begins teaching. His insightful
wisdom astounds the audience.
"The Jews there were amazed and
asked, 'How did this man get such
learning without having been taught?'"
Jesus proclaims that His credo
originates from God. "He who
seeks the glory of the one who sent
Him is a man of truth." Bravely, He
criticizes the Pharisees for attempting
to uphold meticulous rules while
breaking the laws of Moses. Emotions
seethe and pour forth from His
recipients. Some fall to their knees

in anguish as they confess their
sins, others angrily retort that Jesus
is a deceiver or perhaps demonic.
A small faction seeks to kill Him.
Several label Him a prophet and a
good man. What is your reaction
to Jesus' claims? Is He your Messiah,
your Savior, your way, your truth,
your life? May your reaction always
be one of incessant praise. Hallelujah!

Jesus answered, "My teaching is not my own. It comes from the one
who sent me. Anyone who chooses to do the will of God will find
out whether my teaching comes from God or whether I speak on my
own. Whoever speaks on their own does so to gain personal glory, but
he who seeks the glory of the one who sent him is a man of truth;
there is nothing false about him. (John 7:16–18 NIV)

Stoned

Wisps of raven hair dangle about
her frightened face, eyelashes
smudged and cheeks stained with
tears. A crimson sash falls loosely
upon the tattered folds of a pallid
tunic draped across her shoulders.
Thrown to the ground by her captors,
she anxiously awaits her sentence.
The accused adulteress understands
that the punishment for her crime
is death, and this realization is
terrifying. Where is her accomplice?
Why isn't he arrested as stated in
the Jewish law? Why isn't he here
to defend, comfort, and support her
in this dire circumstance? Gazing
upward she hears the allegations
and recoils when she sees the
accusers' eyes glaring. With arms
raised, each palm grips a stone soon
to become a weapon for execution.
The teachers of the law and the Pharisees
declare to Jesus, "'Teacher, this woman
was caught in the act of adultery. In the
law Moses commanded us to stone
such women. Now what do you say?'

They were using this question as a trap
in order to have a basis for accusing Him."
Wondering about the authority of this
stranger, the woman's apprehensive
eyes meet His. Instead of revulsion, she
senses empathy and love. Bending
down, the Savior silently writes in
the soft dirt, and rising, He says, "Let any
one of you who is without sin be the first
to throw a stone ather." One by one,
eldest to youngest, the prosecutors
vacate the premises until there is
none left to convict her. Without
condemnation, Jesus declares,
"Go now and leave your life of sin."
Compassion and forgiveness permeate
this message as Christ illustrates the
perils of judgment. We are to repent
of our sins and ask God for forgiveness.
Similarly, we are to do the same in our
relationship with others. Abandon your
stone and offer a hand. For our author of
justice has reconciled you in His blood and
covered over your sins through His mercy.

When they kept on questioning him, he straightened up and said to them, "Let any one of you who is without sin be the first to throw a stone at her." Again he stooped down and wrote on the ground. At this, those who heard began to go away one at a time, the older ones first, until only Jesus was left, with the woman still standing there. Jesus straightened up and asked her, "Woman, where are they? Has no one condemned you?" "No one, sir," she said. "Then neither do I condemn you," Jesus declared. "Go now and leave your life of sin."(John 8:7–11NIV)

Eyes Wide Open

Dusty and desperate,
the beggar stumbles
against a cracked corner
of a decayed building.
As his hands stroke
the hardened features
of his surroundings,
the cold, gritty surface
assures him of his familiar
whereabouts in this
desolate section of
town where he was born.
Blindness has heightened
his sense of hearing and
in the distance he infers
that a group of Jesus'
disciples are approaching
his domain and questioning
the reason for his blindness.
Their wonderment perpetuates
a discussion as to who had
  sinned;

he in his mother's womb,
or his parents? In response,
cloaked in compassion,
Christ silently creates
a paste of crumbled dirt and
saliva as He covers the eyelids.
When the sightless man
  splashes his face
with the cool waters of the pool
  of Siloam,
miraculously his eyesight is
  restored!
Immediately, colors stream into
  his
line of vision and blurred
objects become clear.
At last he can visualize
the world around him and
unite sound with shape.
A teachable moment allows
God to be glorified through
Christ's benevolent touch.

After saying this, he spit on the ground, made some mud with the saliva, and put it on the man's eyes. 'Go," he told him, "wash in the Pool of Siloam" (this word means "Sent"). So the man went and washed, and came home seeing. (John 9:6–7 NIV)

Hospitality

For days Martha has cooked and cleaned.
Floors are swept, earthenware scrubbed,
and a table is properly set. The cooking,
especially, has been tedious, for the kosher
process is required when serving such a
dignified guest. As the arrival time of her
beloved Jesus becomes imminent, the
pressure increases to have everything in
perfect order. Exhausted and irritated
with her younger sister, Mary, for her
apathy and lack of assistance, she tugs
the heavy cypress door open, heaves a sigh,
and asks Jesus to enter the Bethany home.
Immediately excusing herself from
the conversation, she flees to complete
the daunting number of unfinished tasks
that wait in the kitchen. Peeking past the
curtain that leads to the vestibule,
Martha begrudgingly observes her sister
seated at the rabbi's feet. Attentively,
she listens to His every word. The
tranquility of the situation infuriates
the perturbed hostess. Marching forth,
she demands Jesus educate Mary
on the importance of preparation and
comfort for guests. "Lord, don't you

care that my sister has left me to do
the work by myself? Tell her to help
me!" "Martha, Martha," the Lord answers,
"You are worried and upset about
many things, but few things are needed—or
indeed only one. Mary has chosen what is
better, and it will not be taken away from her."
As a true believer, Martha does care deeply for
Jesus; however, her focus on perfection distracts
her from the joy and wisdom offered by Christ.
It is important to know when to listen
to Jesus and when to act on His behalf. Don't
let your emotions steer your decisions; rather,
rely on the Holy Spirit to direct your course
of action. Welcome Christ into your heart.

But Martha was distracted by all the preparations that had to be
made. She came to him and asked, "Lord, don't you care that my
sister has left me to do the work by myself? Tell her to help me!"
Martha, Martha," the Lord answered, "you are worried and upset
about many things, but few things are needed—or indeed only one.
Mary has chosen what is better, and it will not be taken away from
her." (Luke 10:40–42 NIV)

Detachment

Astute and highly educated,
the scribe spends countless hours
absorbing philosophical information,
reading and transcribing complex
rhetoric, and discussing multifaceted
opinions with resident scholars. His
observations of Jesus and His gospel
are intriguing, and he finds himself
compelled to pursue this religious
practice. With the utmost respect
he implores, "Teacher, I will follow
you wherever you go." It is
obvious to many what an asset
this individual would be to the
ministry, yet he is rebuffed as Jesus
replies, "Foxes have dens and birds
have nests, but the Son of Man
has no place to lay his head."
Our innermost intentions and
motivations are never hidden
from our Lord. Jesus knows that
the scribe's resolute commitment
will quickly dissolve as hardships,
such a lack of comfort, prevail
throughout his weak faith walk. A
sudden conviction without pause

for contemplation will undoubtedly lead to failure. Following Christ is accomplished when we detach ourselves from worldly possessions, the influence of friends and family, and realign our priorities. As we follow our Lord we assume the honor as well as responsibility to serve Him at all costs. In return, Jesus abundantly gives us more than we will ever require. Christ promises that those who are willing to part with what is most dear to them "for my sake will receive a hundred times as much and will inherit eternal life." Separate yourself from insignificant concerns and affix your eyes on the generous Christ who lavishes you with heavenly treasure.

Then a teacher of the law came to him and said, "Teacher, I will follow you wherever you go." Jesus replied, "Foxes have dens and birds have nests, but the Son of Man has no place to lay his head." Another disciple said to him, "Lord, first let me go and bury my father." But Jesus told him, "Follow me, and let the dead bury their own dead."(Matthew 8: 19–22 NIV)

And everyone who has left houses or brothers or sisters or father or mother or wife or children or fields for my sake will receive a hundred times as much and will inherit eternal life. (Matthew 19:29 NIV)

Clad in ebony-shaded veils,
heads are bent and hands clasped as
tears stream down the faces of
the mourners surrounding the
tomb where their beloved brother
and friend, Lazarus, lay for four days.
Admired companion to Jesus, brother
to Mary and Martha, entwined in
faith and fellowship, his departure
is devastating and the loss is great.
Knowing Lazarus's demise is near, Jesus
deliberately arrives following his
hour of death so that the glory of God
can be evidenced by the discerning Jews.
Jesus declares to the sisters that their
dearly loved sibling will rise again.
The rancid stench is overwhelming as
the stone is removed from the dank,
dark entrance to the forbidding cave.
After Jesus bellows his name, Lazarus
emerges, stumbling into the daylight,
wrapped in the grave clothes that adorn
his body, with a cloth concealing his
elated face. Astounded, the witnesses
cannot believe that Lazarus is alive!
The grandeur of God's marvelous power

is extolled, and many become believers
as a result of this incredible miracle.
Jesus shatters death through the triumph
of the resurrection. Dead to flesh,
alive to Christ—a new life is revealed.

When he had said this, Jesus called in a loud voice, "Lazarus, come
out!" The dead man came out, his hands and feet wrapped with strips
of linen, and a cloth around his face. Jesus said to them, "Take off
the grave clothes and let him go." (John 11:43–44 NIV)

Outcast

Having left Galilee for the last time,
Jesus ventures forth to Samaria, a
land inhabited by known enemies
of the Jews. Entering the village,
He is mesmerized by a group of ten
who plead for His help. The frayed
tunics and scruffy beards cannot hide
the erupting lesions that disfigure
each one. Leprosy has ravaged their
bodies and destroyed their lives.
This contagious and incurable
bacteria assails the skin and defeats
the spirit. Banished from friends and
family, the little contact they receive
is absorbed upon the announcement
of their medical status. This audible
label further destroys their dignity.
"When He saw them He said, 'Go
show yourselves to the priests.' And
as they went they were cleaned."
Faith leads to trust and trust leads to
healing. The lepers obediently left
to locate the priests, without being
cured. "They are healed along
the way." One of them, when he saw he
was made well, came back, praising

Jesus in a loud voice. He threw himself
at Jesus' feet and thanked Him. The attitude
of gratitude makes a difference. Humbleness
in mercy allows the believer to appreciate
God's grace. Have you thanked your Lord
today for the many blessings in your life?
Faith + Compliance + Respectful Appreciation
= Spiritual Blessing. Bask in the glory of God!

Jesus asked, "Were not all ten cleansed? Where are the other nine?
Has no one returned to give praise to God except this foreigner?"
Then he said to him, "Rise and go; your faith has made you well."
(Luke 17: 17–19 NIV)

Treetop View

Methodically, the wee man reaches for the sturdy branches that form a series of steps giving rise to the top of the tree. Surveying the horizon, he patiently awaits the arrival of Jesus. This pinnacle view allows the diminutive Zacchaeus an opportunity to witness the teachings of the infamous rabbi as He travels through Jericho—without encountering the obstacle of dense crowds. This solitary setting provides protection from the angry residents who loathe and accuse him of obtaining profits from hefty taxes required by the Roman Empire. Regarded as a thief, he is not even allowed to donate the funds considered to be stolen. Within his heart, Zacchaeus despises his profession but is obliged to continue, which allows him financial independence. Tormented by inner conflict, Zacchaeus longs for peace and has come to seek counsel with the famed Jesus Christ.

Approaching the sycamore tree, Jesus hesitates, gazes upward, and informs Zacchaeus that He will be staying for dinner at his home.

Startled at the request, the tax collector shimmies down the tree, colliding with the dangling, lobed leaves and the spiked fruit clusters as the spectators scowl and complain. Overwhelmed by Jesus' endorsement, he vows to give half of his possessions to the poor and pay back four times the amount to those he swindled. Pleased, Jesus responds, "Today salvation has come to this house, because this man too is a son of Abraham. For the Son of Man came to seek and save what was lost." Christ saves us from ourselves. Invite Him into your heart home today.

But Zacchaeus stood up and said to the Lord, "Look, Lord! Here and now I give half of my possessions to the poor, and if I have cheated anybody out of anything, I will pay back four times the amount." Jesus said to him, "Today salvation has come to this house, because this man, too, is a son of Abraham." (Luke 19:8–9 NIV)

Persecution

Praiseworthy Corridor

Straddled atop a donkey,
Jesus can hear the chorus
of praise in the distance.
He understands their
misguided worship
for a conquering Messiah.
He knows the course
of events that lie ahead,
and they are not
what His followers
anticipate. Brilliant blue
skies and a penetrating sun
form a backdrop for this
halleluiah celebration.
Yet today, instead
of a white horse, as
predicted by the rabbis,
the beloved Jesus
rides a common colt.
Gingerly, the animal
treads across palms
and cloaks strewn
upon the road as a
symbol of reverence.
Gazing at their adoring
faces with love, Jesus
knows His time with them
will be cut short. However,
on this commemorative
corridor of admiration,
Jesus perceives that one
day this shepherd will
indeed return and collect
His sheep on a stallion
befitting a king—for
He is the King of Kings.

They brought the donkey and the colt and placed their cloaks on them for Jesus to sit on. A very large crowd spread their cloaks on the road, while others cut branches from the trees and spread them on the road. The crowds that went ahead of him and those that followed shouted, "Hosanna to the Son of David!"

"Blessed is he who comes in the name of the Lord!"

"Hosanna in the highest heaven!" (Matthew 21:7–9 NIV)

Power

Etched lashes disfigure
the holy body. The severe
beating has left Him
fragile, limp, and afflicted
with pain. A twisted
crown of thorns penetrates
His brow as blood spilled
for our sin trickles across
eyelids lowered in sorrow.
Cloaked in a purple robe,
mocked as the King of Jews,
His tormentors repeatedly
strike Jesus' innocent face.
Isolated, abandoned, and
rejected, He faces His
anticipated fate alone.
The salvation of the world
rests upon this sacrificial
lamb. The open arena
beckons as Jesus is led
in chains into the blinding
sunlight. The dense
crowd congregates during
this preparation of Passover,
awaiting the release of
a condemned prisoner.
Averting blame, Pilate
allows the multitude to
determine the outcome.
A wave of chants, "Crucify,
Crucify," echoes as the
adamant chief priests raise
their fists, marking His doom.
Pulling Jesus aside, the
pompous Pilate whispers,
"Don't you realize I
have power either to
free you or crucify you?"
Jesus answers, "You would
have no power over me if
it were not given to you
from above." Unwavering
in His heavenly authority,
Jesus acknowledges that
the entire regulation
of our lives originates
with God. He has
wondrously created us
and woven together the
details of our existence.
He knows the moment of
our first breath and our
last. We can be assured
that the strength of our
mighty God will dictate our
days now and forever more.

As soon as the chief priests and their officials saw him, they shouted, "Crucify! Crucify!" But Pilate answered, "You take him and crucify him. As for me, I find no basis for a charge against him." The Jewish leaders insisted, "We have a law, and according to that law he must die, because he claimed to be the Son of God." When Pilate heard this, he was even more afraid, and he went back inside the palace. "Where do you come from?" he asked Jesus, but Jesus gave him no answer. Do you refuse to speak to me?" Pilate said. "Don't you realize I have power either to free you or to crucify you?"[1] Jesus answered, "You would have no power over me if it were not given to you from above. Therefore the one who handed me over to you is guilty of a greater sin." (John 19:6–11 NIV)

Lighten the Load

The weight of the heavy cross crushes His already bruised shoulder. Hunched forward, His hands grip the splintered lumber that would soon hold His body. Sweat and blood drip from His brow. Shooting pain radiates throughout a beaten torso. Jesus inhales a breath of courage to forge the path ahead leading to the Place of the Skull, Golgotha. He knows the torture that awaits on that hill of death. With every faltering step, a whip snaps and stings the already ravaged body. Crumbling to the ground, He can go no further. A passerby, Simon of Cyrene, is ordered to carry the cross. Tall and muscular, the healthy foreigner hoists the death chamber and easily completes the journey. Christ comes alongside you and me. He carries our burden and enables us to complete our faith venture successfully. Emmanuel: God is with us.

After they had mocked him, they took off the robe and put his own clothes on him. Then they led him away to crucify him. (Matthew 27:31–32 NIV)

Crossing Over

The nails are pounded
into the human flesh
of God Almighty.
Hoisted above the
collective crowd, the
cross stages the final
chapter of God's
human existence.
Suffocating minute
by minute, our dying
Savior is given wine
vinegar to quench
His parched lips.
Stripped of His clothing
and dignity, He hangs
captured in abominable
suffering. In spite of
His dire circumstances,
once again Jesus cares
for another by offering
redemption to the
remorseful prisoner
suspended by His side.
Drowning in abandonment,
Jesus' anguished wail, "My God,
why have you forsaken me?"
devastates His heavenly
Father to the core. God
turns away, mourning the
passage His son must take
to save an errant world.
A tiny cluster of family and
friends nestle below the
crucified Christ, weeping
uncontrollably. In awe, they
witness Jesus forgive His
executioners, "for they
know not what they are
doing." A pause, a final
breath, a cry—"It is finished"—
and Jesus gives up the
spirit. The momentary silence
quickly becomes a roar
of terror. Earthquakes,
menacing clouds, as well
as thunderous claps of
lightning shake the earth,
reverberating God's anger.
Crypts release the bodies
of the righteous, and they

are raised to life. Screaming spectators attempt to flee the chaotic scene. The veil in the tabernacle, separating man and the Holy of Holies, is torn, allowing access to the great I AM. By crossing over into death, Jesus grants us life.

From noon until three in the afternoon darkness came over all the land. About three in the afternoon Jesus cried out in a loud voice, " (which means "My God, my God, why have you forsaken me?"). When some of those standing there heard this, they said, "He's calling Elijah." Immediately one of them ran and got a sponge. He filled it with wine vinegar, put it on a staff, and offered it to Jesus to drink. The rest said, "Now leave him alone. Let's see if Elijah comes to save him." And when Jesus had cried out again in a loud voice, he gave up his spirit. At that moment the curtain of the temple was torn in two from top to bottom. The earth shook, the rocks split and the tombs broke open. The bodies of many holy people who had died were raised to life. They came out of the tombs after Jesus' resurrection and went into the holy city and appeared to many people. (Matthew 27:45–53 NIV)

Jesus said, "Father, forgive them, for they do not know what they are doing." And they divided up his clothes by casting lots. (Luke 23:34)

Resurrection

The End?

Carefully, Jesus' body is removed
from the cross that framed His
    death.
As friends begin the Jewish
    tradition
of preparation for burial, tears
stream and cries exude anguish.
Their adored companion,
    mentor,
teacher, rabbi, loved one is dead.
Wrapping the delicate linen
    strips around
the once vibrant body leaves them
feeling empty, extremely sad,
confused, and exceedingly afraid.
The fragrance of myrrh and aloe
envelops the air as they

reverently anoint His body.
Cradling Him in their arms,
they transport Jesus to
Joseph's garden tomb.
Here a soft light filters through
the olive trees that shade this
quiet sanctuary of rest.
The dusty path leads the
private processional
to the clay structure
where a darkened doorway
reveals the damp, isolated
domain awaiting the perfect
Son of God.
As the stone seals the opening,
the distraught friends believe
hope is forsaken, all is lost.

Taking Jesus' body, the two of them wrapped it, with the spices, in strips of linen. This was in accordance with Jewish burial customs. At the place where Jesus was crucified, there was a garden, and in the garden a new tomb, in which no one had ever been laid. Because it was the Jewish day of preparation and since the tomb was nearby, they laid Jesus there. (John 19:40–42 NIV)

Resurrected

The heavy darkness
of the early morn
cannot match the
sorrow weighing down
Mary Magdalene's
heart as she shuffles
along the path leading
to the mausoleum.
Grief stricken, Mary
cannot imagine her
life without Jesus.
Hoping to find comfort,
she is compelled to
pray outside His
burial site. As her
tear-filled eyes focus
on the tomb, she is
aghast to see that the
massive stone is
rolled away from
the entrance. Peering
inside, she notices
strips of linen as
well as a pile of
folded cloth that
previously covered
her teacher's head.
Running to the
disciples, Mary conveys
her discovery and
speculates that Jesus'
body has been taken.
Helplessly, she sits
outside the abandoned
chamber and weeps.
Finally, she decides to
take one last look
inside the cold, damp
crypt. Aglow, two
angels sit in tandem
where her loved one
once lay. Turning, she
sees a stranger who
inquires why she is
crying. In response to
her anguished account,
Jesus calls her by name.
"Don't cling to me
for I have not yet
ascended to the Father.

Tell my brothers I am
ascending to my Father
and your Father, to my
God and your God."
Optimistically energized,

Mary flees on a mission
to convey a message
of victory over death.
Jesus has risen! Alleluia!

Now Mary stood outside the tomb crying. As she wept, she bent over to look into the tomb and saw two angels in white, seated where Jesus' body had been, one at the head and the other at the foot. They asked her, "Woman, why are you crying?" "They have taken my Lord away," she said, "and I don't know where they have put him." At this, she turned around and saw Jesus standing there, but she did not realize that it was Jesus. He asked her, "Woman, why are you crying? Who is it you are looking for?" Thinking he was the gardener, she said, "Sir, if you have carried him away, tell me where you have put him, and I will get him." Jesus said to her, "Mary." She turned toward him and cried out in Aramaic, "Rabboni!" (which means "Teacher"). Jesus said, "Do not hold on to me, for I have not yet ascended to the Father. Go instead to my brothers and tell them, 'I am ascending to my Father and your Father, to my God and your God.'" Mary Magdalene went to the disciples with the news: "I have seen the Lord!" And she told them that he had said these things to her. (John 20:11–18 NIV)

Commission

Climbing the rugged terrain of the mountain proves difficult for the grieving eleven disciples. Lost without a leader, confused about the future, and frightened for their safety, they numbly navigate the elevated path to the risen Savior. Having witnessed the resurrection, the followers know the time with Christ is brief and this pilgrimage will reveal His direction for their lives. The rising peak in Galilee is the appointed venue for this elite gathering.

At last, the weary ones arrive at the summit. The authoritative Jesus soon appears. His sympathetic eyes reflect a deep understanding of their pain. Before His final ascension, He offers a command that invigorates their hearts. "Go and make disciples of all nations, baptizing them in the name of the Father and of the Son and of the Holy Spirit and teaching them to obey everything I have commanded you. And surely I am with you always, to the very end of the age." Christ empowers us with the Holy Spirit to seek His will and dutifully spread the gospel to draw others toward His precious truth. As you venture forth into this world, be comforted in knowing that our loving God lives inside you. He will determine your course and provide the strength and means for you to expand His kingdom. You are His light in this world—scatter His love and make a difference.

Therefore go and make disciples of all nations, baptizing them in the name of the Father and of the Son and of the Holy Spirit, and teaching them to obey everything I have commanded you. And surely I am with you always, to the very end of the age." (Matthew 28:19–20 NIV)

About the Author

Nancy Elizabeth Gainor is a retired language arts teacher. Her poetry has been circulated in Lenten books and church publications. Poems of faith, comfort, and reassurance have been written to those seeking God's abundant love, with Scripture at the core of each one. Nancy aspires to "be a light and bring out the God-colors in the world" (Matthew 5:16). Nancy and her husband, John, have three married sons and four grandchildren who are the joy of their life.

CPSIA information can be obtained at www.ICGtesting.com
Printed in the USA
BVOW05s0440110614

355983BV00001B/2/P